SERIFOS

Travel Guide

Discovery

Your all-in-one handbook for discovering hidden gems, top attractions, best beaches, relaxation hotspots, culinary delights, and up-to-date tips.

by

Christopher Morrell

Copyright Notice

This publication is copyright protected. This is only for personal use. No part of this publication may be, including but not limited to, reproduced, in any form or medium, stored in a data retrieval system or transmitted by or through any means, without prior written permission from the Author / Publisher.

Legal action will be pursued if this is breached.

Disclaimer

Please note that the information contained within this document is for educational purposes only. The information contained herein has been obtained from sources believed to be reliable at the time of publication. The opinions expressed herein are subject to change without notice.

Readers acknowledge that the Author / Publisher is not engaging in rendering legal, financial or professional advice. The Publisher / Author disclaims all warranties as to the accuracy, completeness, or adequacy of such information.

The Publisher assumes no liability for errors, omissions, or inadequacies in the information contained herein or from the interpretations thereof. The publisher / Author specifically disclaims any liability from the use or application of the information contained herein or from the interpretations thereof.

Table of Content

Introduction to Serifos 12
    Welcome to Serifos 12
    A Brief History of the Island 12
    Why Serifos is the Perfect Destination 13
    What to Expect from This Guide 14
    Insider Tips from Locals 15

Chapter 1 18
How to Get There 18
    Traveling by Ferry: Ports and Schedules 18
    Flight Options and Nearest Airports 19
    Private Boat and Yacht Charters 21
    Getting to Serifos from Athens 22
    Tips for a Smooth Journey 24

Chapter 2 26
Best Time to Visit and Ideal Duration of Stay 26
    The Four Seasons of Serifos: What to Expect 26
    Best Months for Outdoor Activities 28
    Planning for Festivals and Events 29
    Ideal Length of Stay: Short and Extended Visits 30
    Weather Tips and Packing Essentials 31

Chapter 3 33
Top 10 Must-See Attractions 33
    Chora: The Heart of Serifos 33
    Livadi: The Bustling Port Town 34
    Kastro: Exploring the Ancient Fortress 35
    Psili Ammos Beach: The Island's Crown Jewel 36

Megalo Livadi: Mining History and Scenic Views............37
Monastery of Taxiarches: A Spiritual Journey...............38
Agios Ioannis Beach: Serenity by the Sea......................39
Serifos' Windmills: Icons of the Island..........................40
Archaeological Museum: Discovering the Past.............41
The Old Mines of Serifos: A Step Back in Time..............42

Chapter 4 ....**44**
Practical Information **44**
Currency and Banking: Managing Your Finances...........44
Language and Communication: Getting Around with Ease 46
5.3 Health and Medical Services: Staying Safe.............48
Time Zone and Local Customs 50
Useful Apps and Online Resources 51

Chapter 5 ....**55**
Transportation on Serifos **55**
Public Transport: Buses and Taxis 55
Renting a Car or Scooter: Freedom to Explore 57
Bicycles and Walking: Eco-Friendly Travel....................59
Boat Rentals and Excursions 60
Navigating Serifos: Maps and Tips 62

Chapter 6 ....**65**
Where to Stay: Accommodation Guide **65**
Overview of Accommodation Options 65
Luxury Resorts..65
Budget-Friendly Hotels 66
Boutique Guesthouses 67
Unique Stays 68
Top Recommended Accommodation 69
Choosing the Right Accommodation for You..................70

Booking Tips and Tricks 71

Chapter 7 73
Where to Eat: Culinary Delights 73
Traditional Serifian Dishes: What to Try 73
Top Restaurants in Serifos 74
Best Cafes and Breakfast Spots 76
Where to Find Fresh Seafood 77
Vegetarian and Vegan Options 78
Local Markets and Street Food 79
Wine and Olive Oil Tasting Experiences 80

Chapter 8 82
Exploring Serifos' Beaches 82
Best Beaches for Relaxation 82
Hidden Coves and Secluded Spots 83
Family-Friendly Beaches 84
Beaches for Watersports Enthusiasts 85
How to Get to Remote Beaches 86
Beach Clubs and Facilities 87
Tips for a Perfect Beach Day 89

Chapter 9 90
Cultural and Historical Sites 90
10.1 Serifos' Ancient Sites: Exploring the Past 90
10.2 Churches and Monasteries: Spiritual Heritage 91
Art Galleries and Local Crafts 92
Serifos' Folklore and Traditions 94
Cultural Etiquette: Do's and Don'ts 94
Historical Walking Tours 95
Engaging with Local Artists and Artisans 96

Chapter 10 98

Shopping and Local Markets 98
    Where to Find Authentic Souvenirs 98
    Best Markets for Fresh Produce 99
    Handmade Crafts and Jewelry 101
    Local Boutiques and Shops 102
    Supporting Local Artisans 103
    Bargaining Tips and Market Etiquette 104
    Sustainable Shopping Practices 104

Chapter 11 106
Outdoor Activities and Adventures 106
    Hiking Trails and Scenic Walks 106
    Watersports: Kayaking, Windsurfing, and More 107
    Diving and Snorkeling Spots 108
    Cycling Routes and Tours 109
    Exploring Serifos by Horseback 110
    Rock Climbing and Adventure Sports 110
    Guided Nature Tours and Wildlife Spotting 111

Chapter 12 113
Nightlife and Entertainment in Serifos 113
    Top Bars and Clubs in Serifos 113
    Live Music Venues and Events 115
    Beach Parties and Nightlife by the Sea 116
    Cultural Performances and Theaters 117
    Late-Night Eateries and Cafes 119
    How to Enjoy Serifos' Nightlife Safely 120
    Where to Experience Traditional Greek Dance 121

Chapter 13 123
Festivals and Events in Serifos 123
    Serifos Summer Festival: A Celebration of Culture 123
    Religious Festivals and Local Feasts 123

Music and Arts Festivals 124
Special Events Throughout the Year 125
Participating in Local Traditions 125
Planning Your Trip Around Festivals 126
Tips for Enjoying Festivals Like a Local 127

Chapter 14 129
Day Trips and Nearby Islands 129
Island Hopping: Nearby Cyclades to Explore 129
Day Trip to Sifnos: A Culinary Adventure 130
Visiting Kythnos: Beaches and Hot Springs 131
Sailing Excursions and Private Tours 132
Exploring Smaller Islets by Boat 133
Cultural Day Trips: Art and History 134
Planning a Multi-Island Itinerary 135

Chapter 15 137
Itineraries for Every Traveler 137
Weekend Getaway 137
Cultural Immersion 138
Outdoor Adventure 139
Family-Friendly Trip 139
Budget Travel 140
Solo Traveler's Guide 141
Romantic Getaways 141

Chapter 16 143
Dos and Don'ts on Serifos 143
Respecting Local Customs and Traditions 143
Sustainable and Responsible Travel Practices 144
What to Avoid: Common Tourist Mistakes 145
How to Dress and Behave Appropriately 146
Dos and Don'ts on the Beaches 147

    Navigating Local Laws and Regulations 148
    Tips for Interacting with Locals 149

Chapter 17 151
Sustainable and Responsible Travel 151
    How to Travel Sustainably on Serifos 151
    Supporting Local Communities 152
    Reducing Your Environmental Footprint 152
    Eco-Friendly Accommodation and Dining 153
    Responsible Wildlife and Nature Tours 154
    Ethical Souvenir Shopping 155
    Volunteering Opportunities and Giving Back 156

Chapter 18 157
Health and Safety Tips 157
    Staying Safe on the Beaches and in the Water 157
    Health Precautions and Vaccinations 158
    Emergency Services and Medical Facilities 159
    Tips for Staying Healthy on Your Trip 160
    Safe Food and Water Practices 160
    Avoiding Common Travel Scams 161
    Travel Insurance: Do You Need It? 162

Chapter 19 164
Planning Your Budget 164
    Estimating Your Travel Costs 164
    Saving Money on Accommodation 165
    Dining on a Budget 166
    Affordable Activities and Tours 167
    Transportation Costs and Tips 168
    Shopping Without Breaking the Bank 169
    Managing Your Finances While Traveling 170

Chapter 20 172
Conclusion and Final Tips 172
   Recap of Key Points 172
   Final Travel Tips for an Unforgettable Trip 173
   Encouragement to Explore and Discover 174
   Staying in Touch with Serifos: Social Media and More . 175
   Your Next Adventure: Beyond Serifos 176

Appendix 178
   A. Emergency Contacts 178
   B. Maps and Navigational Tools 178
   Map of things to do in Serifos 179
   C. Additional Reading and References 180
   D. Useful Local Phrases 180
   E. Addresses and Locations of Popular Accommodation 180
   F. Addresses and Locations of Popular Restaurants and Cafes 181
   G. Addresses and Locations of Popular Bars and Clubs 182
   H. Addresses and Locations of Top Attractions 183
   I. Addresses and Locations of Book Shops 183
   J. Addresses and Locations of Top Clinics, Hospitals, and Pharmacies 183
   K. Addresses and Locations of UNESCO World Heritage Sites 184

Map of Serifos

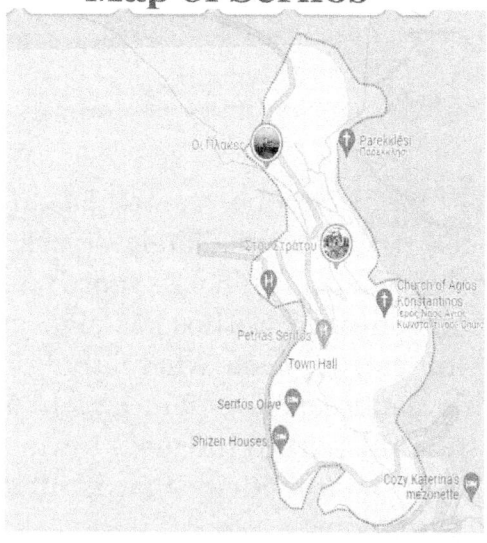

https://maps.app.goo.gl/sbCKzw2dftbEwo7TA

SCAN THE IMAGE/QR CODE WITH YOUR PHONE TO GET THE LOCATIONS IN REAL TIME.

Introduction to Serifos

Welcome to Serifos

When I first set foot on Serifos, a small island nestled in the western Cyclades, I was immediately struck by its rugged beauty and timeless charm. Unlike its more famous neighbors like Mykonos and Santorini, Serifos has managed to maintain a slower pace of life, a place where tradition still reigns supreme, and the landscapes remain largely unspoiled. As I made my way from the port to the main town, or Chora, I felt a sense of peace and authenticity that is often lost in more tourist-heavy destinations.

Serifos is located at approximately 37.1469° N latitude and 24.4886° E longitude. The island is relatively small, covering about 75 square kilometers, but it is packed with hidden treasures waiting to be explored. The island is about 73 nautical miles from the bustling port of Piraeus, making it an easy ferry ride from Athens, yet it feels worlds away from the hustle and bustle of the mainland.

A Brief History of the Island

The history of Serifos is as rich and fascinating as its landscapes. According to Greek mythology, Serifos is where Perseus brought the head of Medusa, and it was here that he saved his mother, Danae, from the clutches of the tyrannical King Polydectes. The island's ancient history is palpable as you explore its archaeological sites and ancient ruins. The remnants of the island's mining past are also evident, with old iron mines dotting the landscape, a testament to Serifos' industrial era in the late 19th and early 20th centuries.

During antiquity, Serifos was known for its iron ore, and it played a significant role in the region's economy. The island's prosperity continued under Venetian rule, and you can still see the influence of this period in the architecture and the fortress-like structures in Chora. Serifos also has a history of resistance; during World War II, it was a stronghold of anti-fascist sentiment, and many of the island's residents joined the resistance against the Axis forces.

Walking through the island's small villages, you can feel the weight of history in the cobblestone streets, the ancient olive groves, and the weathered faces of the locals, who are always eager to share a story or two about their beloved island.

Why Serifos is the Perfect Destination

For me, Serifos represents the perfect escape from the modern world. It's a place where you can truly disconnect and immerse yourself in the simple pleasures of life: pristine beaches, crystal-clear waters, and the warm hospitality of the locals. Unlike the more commercialized islands, Serifos offers a more authentic experience, where you can enjoy traditional Greek life at its finest.

The island is a haven for those who love the outdoors. The rugged terrain is perfect for hiking, and there are numerous trails that take you through the island's stunning landscapes, from the sandy shores to the rocky cliffs. The beaches on Serifos are among the most beautiful I've seen in Greece, with golden sands and turquoise waters that are perfect for swimming, snorkeling, or simply lounging in the sun.

Serifos is also a foodie's paradise. The local cuisine is a delightful blend of fresh seafood, local produce, and traditional recipes passed down through generations. Dining on Serifos is a treat for the senses, whether you're enjoying a simple taverna meal by the sea or indulging in a more elaborate feast in Chora.

But what really makes Serifos special is its people. The locals are warm, welcoming, and proud of their heritage. They are always eager to share their traditions, whether it's through a lively conversation, a local festival, or a homemade meal. It's this sense of community and connection that makes Serifos feel like home, even if you're just visiting for a short time.

What to Expect from This Guide

This guide is my way of sharing my love for Serifos with you. I've spent countless hours exploring the island, getting to know its people, and discovering its hidden gems. Whether you're planning your first trip to Serifos or you're a returning visitor looking for new experiences, this guide is designed to help you make the most of your time on the island.

In the following chapters, I'll take you on a journey through Serifos, from its stunning beaches to its charming villages, its rich history to its vibrant culture. I'll share practical tips on where to stay, where to eat, and what to see, along with insider recommendations from locals who know the island better than anyone.

You'll find detailed information on the island's top attractions, as well as lesser-known spots that are off the beaten path. I'll also provide advice on how to navigate the island, including transportation options, opening hours for key sites, and tips on how to avoid the crowds and enjoy a more peaceful experience.

Insider Tips from Locals

One of the best things about traveling to a place like Serifos is the opportunity to connect with the locals. Over the years, I've made some wonderful friends on the island, and they've been kind enough to share their tips and recommendations with me. Here are a few insider tips that I think will help you experience the best of Serifos:

Timing Your Visit: The best time to visit Serifos is in the late spring or early fall, when the weather is warm but not too hot, and the crowds are smaller. July and August can be quite busy, especially around the main beaches, so if you prefer a quieter experience, plan your trip for May, June, September, or early October.

Exploring Chora: The main town of Chora is best explored on foot. The streets are narrow and steep, so wear comfortable shoes and take your time wandering through the town's labyrinthine alleys. Don't miss the chance to visit the Church of Agios Konstantinos, perched on a hilltop with breathtaking views of the island.

Beach Hopping: Serifos is home to some of the most beautiful beaches in the Cyclades, and each one has its own unique charm. For a more secluded experience, head to beaches like Kalo Ambeli or Vagia, which are less crowded but just as stunning as the more popular spots like Livadakia and Psili Ammos.

Dining Like a Local: When it comes to dining, the locals know best. For an authentic meal, skip the touristy spots and head to a family-run taverna. One of my favorites is Stou Stratou, located in the heart of Chora, where you can enjoy delicious traditional dishes made with fresh, local ingredients. Another great spot is To Bakakaki, known for its grilled meats and homemade desserts.

Cultural Experiences: Serifos is rich in cultural traditions, and there are several festivals and events throughout the year that offer a glimpse into the island's heritage. If you're visiting in August, don't miss the Feast of Panagia, a religious festival that is celebrated with music, dancing, and lots of food.

Getting Around: Renting a car or a scooter is the best way to explore the island at your own pace. The roads are generally in good condition, but they can be steep and winding, so drive carefully. If you prefer not to drive, there are also local buses that connect the main villages and beaches.

Staying Safe: Serifos is a safe and welcoming destination, but it's always a good idea to take basic precautions. Keep an eye on your belongings, especially in crowded areas, and be respectful of the local customs and traditions.

Serifos is a place that stays with you long after you've left. It's an island that invites you to slow down, soak in the natural beauty, and connect with the local culture. I hope this guide helps you discover the magic of Serifos and inspires you to create your own unforgettable memories on this incredible island.

Chapter 1

How to Get There

Traveling by Ferry: Ports and Schedules

When I first set my eyes on Serifos, it was after a soothing ferry ride from Piraeus, the bustling port of Athens. There's something magical about approaching an island by sea—the salty breeze, the anticipation, and then, there it is: Serifos, a rugged beauty rising from the Aegean Sea.

Serifos is well-connected by ferry, with several routes departing daily from Piraeus, especially during the summer months when tourism peaks. The ferry ride takes around 2 to 5 hours, depending on the type of ferry—high-speed or regular. High-speed ferries are faster, getting you there in about 2 hours, but they tend to be a bit pricier. I personally enjoyed the regular ferry, where I could relax on the deck and take in the endless blue sea.

The port town of Livadi is where you'll dock. It's a charming little place with whitewashed buildings, lively cafes, and the backdrop of Chora, Serifos' capital, perched high on a hill. When you disembark, you're right in the thick of it, with everything from rental agencies to local eateries just a stone's throw away.

Opening hours: Ferries operate typically from early morning until late evening, with the first ferry often leaving around 7:00 AM.

Coordinates: 37.1396° N, 24.5172° E

Address: Livadi Port, Serifos 840 05, Greece

Contact: The best way to check schedules and book tickets is through ferry companies like Blue Star Ferries or SeaJets. You can also contact local agencies in Livadi for updated schedules.

Phone Number: +30 210 891 9800 (Piraeus Port Authority)

Price range: Tickets range from €20 to €50 for economy class, depending on the ferry type and season.

Website: www.bluestarferries.com | www.seajets.gr

Flight Options and Nearest Airports

Now, here's the thing Serifos doesn't have its own airport. This might sound like a hassle, but trust me, it's part of what keeps the island so blissfully unspoiled. The nearest airports are on the neighboring islands of Milos or Syros, or even on the mainland in Athens.

During one of my trips, I opted to fly into Milos Island National Airport (MLO), which is about 37 nautical miles from Serifos. The flight from Athens to Milos is quick, about 40 minutes, and from there, you can catch a ferry to Serifos.

The ferry ride from Milos to Serifos takes about 2 hours, and it's a scenic route.

If you choose to fly into Syros (Syros Island National Airport - JMK), it's another option. The airport is slightly further away, and the ferry ride from Syros to Serifos takes around 3 hours.

But if you're looking for convenience, flying into Athens International Airport (ATH) and then taking a ferry from Piraeus is your best bet. It's the most straightforward route, and the airport in Athens has all the amenities you could need, including frequent flights from major cities around the world.

Opening hours: Airports are generally open 24/7, with flight times varying.

Coordinates:

Milos Airport: 36.6966° N, 24.4763° E

Syros Airport: 37.4229° N, 24.9509° E

Athens Airport: 37.9364° N, 23.9475° E

Address:

Milos Airport: 848 00, Milos, Greece

Syros Airport: Syros 841 00, Greece

Athens Airport: Spata Loutsa 190 04, Greece

Contact: For flight bookings and inquiries, contact the respective airlines or the airport information desks.

Phone Number:

Milos Airport: +30 22870 28851

Syros Airport: +30 22810 81900

Athens Airport: +30 210 353 0000

Price range: Flights from Athens to Milos or Syros range from €60 to €120 depending on the airline and time of booking.

Website: www.aia.gr | www.olympicair.com

Private Boat and Yacht Charters

For those looking for a more luxurious and private arrival, chartering a boat or yacht is an incredible way to reach Serifos. I remember the time I splurged on a yacht charter with some friends—it was an experience of pure indulgence. There's nothing like cruising the Aegean at your own pace, stopping at secluded coves and diving into crystal-clear waters whenever you fancy.

Several companies in Athens and the nearby islands offer private boat and yacht charters that can take you directly to Serifos. You can choose from various options, from sailboats to motor yachts, depending on your budget and group size. Most charters come with a skipper, but if you're licensed, you might prefer to take the helm yourself.

Once you arrive, you can dock at Livadi Port, which has facilities for yachts, including water and electricity. This option gives you the freedom to explore the island and the surrounding Cyclades at your leisure.

Opening hours: Charters typically operate from morning until late evening, depending on the arrangements.

Coordinates: 37.1396° N, 24.5172° E (Livadi Port)

Address: Livadi Port, Serifos 840 05, Greece

Contact: Various yacht charter companies operate from Athens and nearby islands.

Phone Number: It's best to contact your preferred charter company directly for pricing and availability.

Price range: Prices for a yacht charter can range from €1,000 to €10,000 per day, depending on the type of boat and services included.

Website: www.istion.com | www.greececharters.com

Getting to Serifos from Athens

Athens, the gateway to the Greek islands, is where most travelers begin their journey to Serifos. I've done this route a few times, and each time it feels like the start of a new adventure. From Athens, you'll need to make your way to Piraeus, the city's main port.

Getting to Piraeus from Athens International Airport is straightforward. You can take the direct metro line (Line 3 to Monastiraki, then Line 1 to Piraeus) or catch an express bus (X96) that runs 24/7. The metro is faster, taking about an hour, while the bus might take up to 90 minutes, depending on traffic.

If you're already in the city center, the metro or a quick taxi ride will get you to Piraeus in no time. Once at the port, it's easy to find your ferry—there are clear signs, and the ticket offices are just a short walk from the metro station. I usually like to arrive early, grab a coffee at one of the nearby cafes, and watch the hustle and bustle of the port.

From Piraeus, the ferry to Serifos is a comfortable journey. You can relax in the lounge, grab a bite to eat, or simply enjoy the view as you sail past other Cycladic islands like Kythnos and Kea.

Opening hours: Metro and bus services operate daily, with the metro starting at 5:30 AM and the bus running 24/7.

Coordinates:

Piraeus Port: 37.9411° N, 23.6465° E

Athens Airport: 37.9364° N, 23.9475° E

Address:

Piraeus Port: Akti Miaouli 10, Piraeus 185 38, Greece

Athens Airport: Spata Loutsa 190 04, Greece

Contact: The metro and bus services have information desks at the airport and major stations.

Phone Number:

Athens Metro: +30 214 414 6400

Piraeus Port Authority: +30 210 891 9800

Price range: Metro tickets from the airport to Piraeus cost around €10, while the bus fare is approximately €6.

Website: www.stasy.gr | www.oasa.gr

Tips for a Smooth Journey

Having traveled to Serifos multiple times, I've picked up a few tips and tricks to make the journey as smooth as possible. First off, if you're prone to seasickness, consider taking some motion sickness tablets before the ferry ride—it can get a bit choppy, especially on the slower ferries.

Booking your ferry tickets in advance is always a good idea, particularly during the high season (July and August). The ferries can get crowded, and securing your spot early ensures you won't be left scrambling for a seat.

I also recommend packing light, especially if you're taking the metro or bus to Piraeus. Navigating the port with heavy luggage can be a hassle, and once you're on Serifos, you'll likely be moving around a lot, exploring different beaches and villages.

Another handy tip is to download offline maps of Serifos before you go. Although the island has decent mobile coverage, some areas can be a bit patchy, and having a map on hand will make it easier to navigate the winding roads and hiking trails.

Lastly, embrace the slower pace of island life. Things might not always run on time—ferries can be delayed, and buses might not arrive when expected—but that's part of the charm. Serifos is an island where time seems to stand still, and once you adjust to its rhythm, you'll find yourself falling in love with its laid-back vibe.

Traveling to Serifos is an experience in itself, filled with anticipation and the promise of discovery. Whether you're arriving by ferry, flight, or yacht, the journey sets the stage for the wonders that await on this enchanting island.

Chapter 2

Best Time to Visit and Ideal Duration of Stay

The Four Seasons of Serifos: What to Expect

Serifos, like many of the Cycladic islands, experiences a Mediterranean climate, which means mild, wet winters and hot, dry summers. However, each season on Serifos brings its own unique charm, and the island's landscape and atmosphere change subtly as the months pass.

Spring (March to May):

Springtime in Serifos is a season of renewal. The island's hillsides are blanketed in vibrant green, and wildflowers bloom in abundance, creating a picturesque setting for outdoor exploration. The weather is generally mild, with temperatures ranging from 15°C (59°F) in March to 22°C (72°F) in May. This is one of the best times to visit if you enjoy hiking or simply want to experience the island without the summer crowds. The sea might still be a bit chilly for swimming, but the sunny days and cool breezes make it ideal for walking and sightseeing.

Summer (June to August):

Summer is the peak tourist season in Serifos, and for good reason. The weather is warm and sunny, with average temperatures ranging from 25°C (77°F) in June to 30°C (86°F) in August. The island's beaches are at their most inviting, and the clear, turquoise waters are perfect for swimming, snorkeling, and other water activities. While it can get hot, especially in July and August, the island's constant breeze, known as the "Meltemi," helps to keep things comfortable. Keep in mind that this is also the busiest time of year, so popular spots like Livadakia Beach and Psili Ammos can get crowded.

Autumn (September to November):

Autumn is another excellent time to visit Serifos. The crowds start to thin out, but the weather remains warm, especially in September and early October. Temperatures during this time range from 24°C (75°F) in September to 18°C (64°F) in November. The sea is still warm from the summer sun, making it perfect for swimming. As the season progresses, the island takes on a more tranquil vibe, and the changing colors of the landscape add a different kind of beauty. This is a great time for those who prefer a quieter, more relaxed experience.

Winter (December to February):

Winter is the quietest season on Serifos, and while it's not the ideal time for beach activities, it offers a different perspective of the island. Temperatures range from 10°C (50°F) to 15°C (59°F), and while it can be rainy and windy, there are also plenty of sunny days. This is the time to experience Serifos at its most authentic, as the island returns to its traditional rhythms. Many of the tourist amenities may be closed, but the local tavernas and shops that remain open offer a warm welcome. Winter is perfect for those who want to immerse themselves in the local culture and enjoy a peaceful retreat.

Best Months for Outdoor Activities

If you're coming to Serifos to enjoy the great outdoors, the best months to visit are May, June, September, and October. These months offer a perfect balance of pleasant weather and fewer crowds, making it easier to explore the island's natural beauty.

Hiking: The spring and autumn months are ideal for hiking, with temperatures that are comfortable for long walks. The island is crisscrossed with trails that take you through its rugged terrain, offering stunning views of the Aegean Sea and the surrounding islands. One of my favorite hikes is the trail from Chora to Kastro, where you can explore the ruins of the old Venetian fortress.

Beach Activities: For those who want to spend their days by the sea, June and September are perfect. The water is warm enough for swimming, and the beaches are less crowded than during the peak summer months. I particularly enjoy the beach at Vagia, which is a bit more secluded and offers a tranquil setting.

Water Sports: If you're into windsurfing or kiteboarding, the summer months of July and August are best, as the Meltemi winds pick up during this time, providing excellent conditions for these sports.

Photography: If you're a photography enthusiast, spring and autumn offer the best lighting and the most striking contrasts. The island's natural beauty is at its peak, and the soft light of the early morning and late afternoon is perfect for capturing stunning images.

Planning for Festivals and Events

Serifos is a place where traditions are alive and well, and the island hosts several festivals and events throughout the year that provide a unique insight into the local culture. If you're interested in experiencing these celebrations, it's worth planning your visit around them.

The Feast of Panagia (August 15th): This is the biggest religious festival on the island, dedicated to the Virgin Mary. It's held in Chora and involves a church service followed by traditional music, dancing, and a feast that lasts well into the night. It's a wonderful opportunity to experience the island's culture and meet the locals.

Serifos Sunset Race (Late August): This is a relatively new event that has quickly become popular. It's a road race that takes place during sunset, offering participants breathtaking views as they run along the island's coastal roads. There's also a swimming race held on the same day, making it a great event for sports enthusiasts.

Fishermen's Festival (July): Held in the port of Livadi, this festival celebrates the island's fishing heritage. It's a lively event with plenty of seafood, traditional music, and dancing. It's a great way to enjoy the local cuisine and experience Serifos' maritime traditions.

The Wine Festival (September): Serifos has a long history of winemaking, and this festival celebrates the island's wines with tastings, music, and dancing. It's held in the village of Koutalas, and it's a great way to sample some of the island's best wines and learn about its viticulture.

Ideal Length of Stay: Short and Extended Visits

Deciding how long to stay on Serifos depends on what you want to get out of your visit. Whether you're looking for a quick escape or a longer, more immersive experience, Serifos has something to offer.

Short Stay (3-4 Days):

If you're on a tight schedule but still want to experience the best of Serifos, a three to four-day stay can be enough to cover the highlights. Spend your first day exploring Chora, with its narrow alleys, whitewashed houses, and stunning views. On your second day, visit some of the island's most beautiful beaches, such as Livadakia and Psili Ammos. On the third day, take a hike to Kastro and explore the ancient ruins, and if you have a fourth day, consider taking a boat tour around the island to see some of the more remote beaches and coves.

Extended Stay (7-10 Days):

For a more relaxed and in-depth experience, I recommend spending a week or more on Serifos. This will give you time to explore the island at a leisurely pace and really soak in its atmosphere. With a longer stay, you can visit more of the island's villages, each with its own unique character. You'll have time to enjoy multiple beaches, go on several hikes, and perhaps even take a day trip to a nearby island. An extended stay also allows you to experience more of the local culture, especially if you time your visit to coincide with one of the island's festivals.

Weather Tips and Packing Essentials

Preparing for your trip to Serifos involves packing wisely, especially considering the island's varying weather conditions throughout the year.

Spring and Autumn:

If you're visiting in the spring or autumn, pack layers. The days can be warm, but the evenings may be cooler, especially in the higher elevations like Chora. A light jacket or sweater will be useful. Comfortable walking shoes are a must if you plan on hiking, as the terrain can be rocky. Don't forget sunscreen and a hat, as the sun can still be quite strong.

Summer:

For summer visits, light, breathable clothing is key. The temperatures can get quite high, so pack plenty of sun protection, including sunscreen, a wide-brimmed hat, and sunglasses. A swimsuit is essential, as you'll likely be spending a lot of time at the beach. Flip-flops are fine for the beach, but if you plan on exploring the town or hiking, you'll need sturdy sandals or shoes. A reusable water bottle is a good idea to stay hydrated throughout the day.

Winter:

In winter, the weather can be unpredictable, so pack for cooler temperatures and the possibility of rain. A waterproof jacket and warmer clothing like sweaters and long pants are necessary. While you might not be spending much time on the beach, there are still plenty of opportunities to explore the island, so comfortable shoes are still important.

Year-Round Essentials:

Regardless of when you visit, there are a few items that are always good to have on hand. A travel-sized first aid kit, insect repellent, and a power bank for your devices can be lifesavers. A good guidebook or a downloaded map of the island is also handy, as mobile reception can be spotty in some areas. And of course, don't forget your camera to capture the stunning beauty of Serifos.

Serifos is a destination that rewards careful planning, but it's also a place where you can let go of the itinerary and simply enjoy the moment. Whether you're here for a few days or a few weeks, you'll find that the island's natural beauty, rich history, and warm hospitality will leave a lasting impression.

Chapter 3

Top 10 Must-See Attractions

Serifos, a hidden gem in the Cyclades, is rich in history, culture, and natural beauty. Each attraction on this island tells a unique story, blending the island's ancient past with its serene landscapes. Having spent some time wandering through its charming towns and exploring its breathtaking sites, I can confidently say that these ten attractions should be at the top of anyone's Serifos itinerary.

Chora: The Heart of Serifos

Chora is the quintessential Greek island town, perched on a hill with whitewashed houses, narrow alleyways, and stunning views of the Aegean Sea. When I first arrived in Chora, I was immediately struck by its timeless beauty. The town feels like a place where history and daily life effortlessly intertwine. Walking through its winding streets, I discovered small cafes, artisanal shops, and hidden squares where locals gathered to chat and enjoy a coffee.

The heart of Chora is its main square, Plateia. Here, you'll find the Town Hall, an elegant building that dates back to the early 20th century. The square is a great place to sit and people-watch or enjoy a traditional Greek meal at one of the nearby tavernas.

One of the highlights of Chora is the Church of Agios Konstantinos, located at the highest point of the town. The panoramic views from here are breathtaking, especially at sunset. The coordinates for Chora are 37.1472° N, 24.4996° E.

Opening Hours: Always accessible

Coordinates: 37.1472° N, 24.4996° E

Address: Chora, Serifos 84005, Greece

Contact: Not applicable

Price Range: Free

Website Address: Not applicable

Livadi: The Bustling Port Town

Livadi is the main port town of Serifos, and it's where most visitors will first set foot on the island. The town is lively and vibrant, with a variety of cafes, restaurants, and shops lining the waterfront. I spent many evenings here, watching the boats come and go while enjoying a glass of local wine. The beach at Livadi is long and sandy, making it a great spot for a relaxing swim. The shallow waters are perfect for families with young children. Livadi is also a hub for transportation on the island, with buses and taxis readily available to take you to other parts of Serifos.

One of my favorite experiences in Livadi was taking a stroll along the pier at sunset. The light reflecting off the water, with the hills of Serifos in the background, created a magical atmosphere. If you're a seafood lover, you'll find plenty of fresh catches served at the waterfront tavernas.

Opening Hours: Always accessible

Coordinates: 37.1422° N, 24.4828° E

Address: Livadi, Serifos 84005, Greece

Contact: Not applicable

Price Range: Free

Website Address: Not applicable

Kastro: Exploring the Ancient Fortress

The Kastro, or Castle, of Serifos is a must-see for anyone interested in the island's history. This ancient fortress sits at the top of Chora, offering commanding views of the surrounding area. The climb to the Kastro is steep, but it's well worth the effort. As I made my way up, I could almost imagine the ancient defenders of the island standing guard, watching for approaching ships.

The Kastro dates back to the medieval period, and while much of it is in ruins, the sense of history is palpable. The view from the top is truly spectacular, with a panoramic vista that takes in the Aegean Sea, the nearby islands, and the rugged landscape of Serifos.

Walking through the remains of the fortress, I found myself reflecting on the island's long history of conquest and defense. It's a place that invites contemplation and offers a deeper understanding of Serifos's past.

Opening Hours: Always accessible

Coordinates: 37.1453° N, 24.4999° E

Address: Chora, Serifos 84005, Greece

Contact: Not applicable

Price Range: Free

Website Address: Not applicable

Psili Ammos Beach: The Island's Crown Jewel

Psili Ammos Beach is often regarded as the most beautiful beach on Serifos, and after spending a day there, I can see why. The sand is soft and golden, and the waters are crystal clear, with shades of turquoise that seem almost unreal. It's the perfect spot for a day of relaxation.

When I visited Psili Ammos, I found the beach to be relatively quiet, even in the peak of summer. There are a few tavernas nearby where you can grab a bite to eat or a cold drink, but the beach itself is largely unspoiled. I spent hours swimming in the calm waters and lounging on the sand, soaking up the sun.

The beach is located on the eastern side of the island, and while it's a bit of a trek to get there, it's absolutely worth it. The coordinates for Psili Ammos Beach are 37.1509° N, 24.5182° E.

Opening Hours: Always accessible

Coordinates: 37.1509° N, 24.5182° E

Address: Psili Ammos, Serifos 84005, Greece

Contact: Not applicable

Price Range: Free

Website Address: Not applicable

Megalo Livadi: Mining History and Scenic Views

Megalo Livadi is a small village on the southwest coast of Serifos, known for its rich mining history. The village was once a thriving mining town, and many of the old buildings and equipment still remain, giving it a slightly eerie, yet fascinating, atmosphere. I was particularly struck by the contrast between the beautiful natural surroundings and the remnants of the industrial past.

The old mining facilities are still visible, and you can even see the old ore-loading dock extending into the sea. Walking through the village, I felt like I was stepping back in time. The history here is tangible, and it's easy to imagine what life must have been like when the mines were in full operation. Megalo Livadi is also home to a lovely beach, and after exploring the mining sites, I took a dip in the sea to cool off. The village is quiet and peaceful, making it a great place to unwind and reflect on the island's past.

Opening Hours: Always accessible

Coordinates: 37.1267° N, 24.4541° E

Address: Megalo Livadi, Serifos 84005, Greece

Contact: Not applicable

Price Range: Free

Website Address: Not applicable

Monastery of Taxiarches: A Spiritual Journey

The Monastery of Taxiarches, located in the northern part of Serifos, is one of the island's most important religious sites. The monastery is dedicated to the Archangels Michael and

Gabriel, who are the patron saints of Serifos. Visiting the monastery was a deeply moving experience for me, not only because of its spiritual significance but also because of its stunning architecture and serene surroundings. The monastery was built in the 16th century and has a fortress-like appearance, with thick walls and narrow windows designed to protect it from pirate attacks. Inside, you'll find beautiful frescoes and icons, some of which date back to the Byzantine period. The peace and quiet of the monastery are truly captivating, and I found it to be a perfect place for reflection. The views from the monastery are also spectacular, with the rugged landscape of Serifos stretching out before you. It's a bit of a drive to get there, but the journey is part of the experience. The coordinates for the Monastery of Taxiarches are 37.1772° N, 24.4867° E.

Opening Hours: Daily, 9:00 AM - 6:00 PM

Coordinates: 37.1772° N, 24.4867° E

Address: Monastery of Taxiarches, Serifos 84005, Greece

Contact: +30 2281 051228

Price Range: Free

Website Address: Not applicable

Agios Ioannis Beach: Serenity by the Sea

Agios Ioannis Beach is one of those hidden gems that you might miss if you're not looking for it, but it's well worth seeking out. Located on the southeastern coast of Serifos, this beach is a true haven of tranquility. The beach is small and secluded, with golden sand and clear, shallow waters. I spent a peaceful afternoon here, away from the crowds, just enjoying the sound of the waves and the warmth of the sun. The beach is named after the small chapel of Agios Ioannis, which sits on a hill overlooking the sea. The chapel adds to the beach's charm and provides a great spot for photos. Agios Ioannis is a bit off the beaten path, so it's perfect for those who want to escape the busier beaches and enjoy some quiet time in nature.

Opening Hours: Always accessible

Coordinates: 37.1315° N, 24.5264° E

Address: Agios Ioannis Beach, Serifos 84005, Greece

Contact: Not applicable

Price Range: Free

Website Address: Not applicable

Serifos' Windmills: Icons of the Island

The windmills of Serifos are iconic symbols of the island, and no visit would be complete without seeing them up close.

These windmills are scattered across the island, but some of the best-preserved examples can be found near Chora. I was fascinated by these structures, which have been a part of the island's landscape for centuries. The windmills were originally used to grind grain, and while they are no longer in operation, they stand as a testament to the island's agricultural past. The views from the windmills are incredible, with sweeping panoramas of the Aegean Sea and the surrounding hills. I spent a quiet afternoon exploring the windmills, imagining what life must have been like for the people who once relied on them. It's a peaceful place, perfect for a leisurely walk and some contemplation.

Opening Hours: Always accessible

Coordinates: 37.1472° N, 24.4996° E

Address: Near Chora, Serifos 84005, Greece

Contact: Not applicable

Price Range: Free

Website Address: Not applicable

Archaeological Museum: Discovering the Past

The Archaeological Museum of Serifos is a small but fascinating museum located in Chora. It's a must-visit for anyone interested in the island's history. The museum houses a collection of artifacts from various periods, including the prehistoric, classical, and Byzantine eras. I was particularly impressed by the pottery and sculptures on display, which provide a glimpse into the daily life of ancient Serifos. The museum is well-organized, with informative displays that explain the significance of each artifact. I found it to be a great way to learn more about the island's rich history, and it added a deeper dimension to my exploration of Serifos.

Opening Hours: Tuesday - Sunday, 8:30 AM - 3:00 PM

Coordinates: 37.1469° N, 24.4992° E

Address: Chora, Serifos 84005, Greece

Contact: +30 2281 051231

Price Range: €4 per person

Website Address: Not applicable

The Old Mines of Serifos: A Step Back in Time

The old mines of Serifos are a fascinating part of the island's industrial heritage. Located near Megalo Livadi, these mines were once the center of a thriving mining industry that played a significant role in the island's economy. Today, the remnants of the mines are a haunting reminder of Serifos's past.

Visiting the old mines was one of the most memorable experiences of my time on Serifos. The area is dotted with abandoned mining equipment, rusted tracks, and dilapidated buildings. It's a place where nature has slowly begun to reclaim the land, and the juxtaposition of the industrial ruins with the surrounding natural beauty is striking. Walking through the mines, I couldn't help but think about the people who worked here, often in harsh conditions. The old mines are a poignant reminder of the island's history and a unique place to explore.

Opening Hours: Always accessible

Coordinates: 37.1267° N, 24.4541° E

Address: Near Megalo Livadi, Serifos 84005, Greece

Contact: Not applicable

Price Range: Free

Website Address: Not applicable

These ten attractions offer a diverse and enriching experience of Serifos, from its vibrant towns to its serene beaches, and from its ancient ruins to its spiritual sites. Each location has left a lasting impression on me, and I hope they do the same for you as you explore this beautiful island.

Chapter 4

Practical Information

Currency and Banking: Managing Your Finances

When I first set foot on Serifos, one of the things I quickly realized was how important it is to have a good handle on my finances while exploring this charming island. Like the rest of Greece, the official currency here is the Euro (€), and it's essential to have cash on hand, especially when visiting smaller villages or more remote areas where card payments might not always be an option.

Currency Exchange:

If you're arriving from outside the Eurozone, you'll need to exchange your currency. While there are no currency exchange offices on the island itself, you can exchange your money at major banks in Athens before you head to Serifos. I found that the most convenient option is to withdraw Euros directly from an ATM once you're on the island.

ATMs:

ATMs are available in the main areas like Chora and Livadi. I remember using the ATM near the port in Livadi on multiple occasions, and it was always reliable. Just keep in mind that some of the smaller villages may not have an ATM, so plan accordingly. It's also worth noting that ATMs can sometimes run out of cash during peak tourist seasons, so it's wise to withdraw what you need early in the day.

Banks and Opening Hours:

The primary bank on the island is the National Bank of Greece, located in Livadi. The bank's opening hours are typically from 8:00 AM to 2:00 PM, Monday through Friday. On my visit, I had to make a quick stop at the bank, and I was pleasantly surprised by the helpfulness of the staff, even though English wasn't widely spoken.

Bank Address:

National Bank of Greece

Livadi, Serifos

Coordinates: 37.1459° N, 24.4871° E

Phone Number: +30 22810 51490

Price Range:

Currency exchange rates vary depending on the bank and service fees. ATMs generally charge a fee for withdrawals, typically around €2-€4 per transaction.

Budgeting Tip:

I found that budgeting around €50-€100 per day was reasonable, depending on whether I was dining out frequently or indulging in activities like boat rentals. Having a mix of cash and card is ideal.

Language and Communication: Getting Around with Ease

Greek is the official language on Serifos, and while many locals speak English, especially in tourist-heavy areas like Livadi and Chora, it's always appreciated when visitors make an effort to learn a few basic Greek phrases. I found that just knowing how to say "hello" (γεια σας - yia sas) and "thank you" (ευχαριστώ - efharistó) made interactions smoother and more enjoyable.

Language:

In more rural parts of the island, I encountered a few older locals who spoke little to no English. In those moments, I relied on hand gestures and a smile, which always seemed to work. For those who want to dive a bit deeper, there are language apps that can help you pick up some conversational Greek before your trip.

Useful Phrases:

Hello: γεια σας (yia sas)

Goodbye: αντίο (antío)

Please: παρακαλώ (parakaló)

Thank you: ευχαριστώ (efharistó)

Yes: ναι (ne)

No: όχι (óchi)

How much does this cost?: Πόσο κοστίζει αυτό; (Póso kostízei aftó?)

Communication Tips:

During my time on the island, I often used a combination of English and basic Greek phrases. I noticed that the locals genuinely appreciated the effort and were more willing to help. For instance, in a small taverna in Megalo Livadi, the owner was so delighted with my attempt at Greek that he offered me a free dessert!

Mobile Coverage:

Mobile coverage is generally good across Serifos, especially in main towns and popular beaches. However, in more remote areas like some of the island's hidden coves, the signal can be patchy. I found it useful to download offline maps and guides before heading out on day trips.

SIM Cards:

If you're planning to stay on the island for a while, consider purchasing a local SIM card for better rates on calls and data. These can be bought in Athens before you arrive on Serifos, or from kiosks in Livadi.

Price Range:

SIM cards usually cost around €10-€20, with data plans available for an additional €5-€20, depending on your needs.

5.3 Health and Medical Services: Staying Safe

While Serifos is a small island, it's reassuring to know that there are medical services available should you need them. During my visit, I didn't have to use any medical services, but I made sure to note the locations and numbers, just in case.

Health Centers:

The main health center on Serifos is located in Livadi. It's a small facility, but the staff are trained to handle emergencies and common medical issues. For anything more serious, patients are typically transferred to larger hospitals in Athens.

Health Center Address:

Health Center of Serifos

Livadi, Serifos

Coordinates: 37.1435° N, 24.4895° E

Phone Number: +30 22810 51202

Pharmacies:

There are a couple of pharmacies on the island, primarily in Livadi and Chora. I found the pharmacists to be knowledgeable and helpful. Whether you need something for a sunburn or a pesky mosquito bite, they've got you covered.

Pharmacy Address:

Pharmacy of Serifos

Livadi, Serifos

Coordinates: 37.1447° N, 24.4890° E

Phone Number: +30 22810 51223

Opening Hours:

Health centers and pharmacies generally operate from 8:00 AM to 2:00 PM, Monday through Friday. Pharmacies may have reduced hours on weekends, so it's best to stock up on essentials during the week.

Emergency Numbers:

General Emergency: 112

Police: 100

Ambulance: 166

Fire Department: 199

Price Range:

Medical services for tourists are usually provided at a reasonable cost, though it's always a good idea to have travel insurance that covers medical emergencies.

Travel Tip:

I carried a small first-aid kit with me, which included band-aids, antiseptic cream, painkillers, and antihistamines. It came in handy after a day of hiking when I needed to treat a blister.

Time Zone and Local Customs

Serifos, like the rest of Greece, operates on Eastern European Time (EET) during the winter months, which is UTC +2, and Eastern European Summer Time (EEST) during the summer, which is UTC +3. Knowing the time zone is essential for planning your activities, especially if you're coordinating with others in different time zones.

Time Zone:

Standard Time: UTC +2

Daylight Saving Time: UTC +3

Local Customs:

One of the things I love about Serifos is the laid-back lifestyle. The island operates on "island time," meaning that things move at a slower pace. Don't be surprised if shops open late in the morning and close for a few hours in the afternoon for siesta, only to reopen in the evening.

Cultural Etiquette:

Greeks are known for their hospitality, and Serifos is no different. During my stay, I was invited into homes for coffee and pastries on more than one occasion, simply because I had taken the time to chat with locals. It's customary to greet people with a smile and a "yia sas" when entering a shop or restaurant.

Dress Code:

While the island is fairly relaxed, it's respectful to dress modestly when visiting churches or religious sites. I always carried a lightweight scarf in my bag, which I could use to cover my shoulders if needed.

Dining Etiquette:

When dining out, I noticed that meals are a leisurely affair. It's common to spend several hours enjoying food, wine, and conversation. Tipping is appreciated but not mandatory; I usually left around 5-10% of the bill as a thank you for excellent service.

Important Note:

Always remember that the water in Serifos is not drinkable from the tap. I learned this the hard way after filling my bottle at the hotel. Stick to bottled water, which is widely available and inexpensive.

Price Range:

Local customs don't typically incur costs, but it's worth budgeting for tips in restaurants and cafes.

Useful Apps and Online Resources

During my travels on Serifos, I relied on a handful of apps and online resources to make my trip smoother and more enjoyable. Here's what I found most useful:

Google Maps:

This was my go-to for navigating the island. I downloaded the map of Serifos for offline use, which was incredibly handy in areas where mobile signal was weak. The coordinates feature also allowed me to pinpoint specific locations with ease.

Maps Coordinates:

For Serifos, I noted the following coordinates for key areas:

Livadi: 37.1438° N, 24.4900° E

Chora: 37.1504° N, 24.4875° E

Psili Ammos Beach: 37.1620° N, 24.4990° E

Price Range:

Google Maps is free to use, though data charges may apply if you're not on Wi-Fi.

Greek-English Translator:

Given that not everyone on the island speaks English fluently, this app was a lifesaver for communicating with locals. I particularly liked the voice-to-text feature, which helped with pronunciations.

Price Range:

Free versions are available with ads, or you can purchase a premium version for around €5-€10.

Booking.com:

This app was essential for finding and booking accommodation on the go. I liked that I could filter options based on my budget and preferences, such as proximity to the beach or amenities like Wi-Fi.

Price Range:

Free to download, with accommodation prices varying widely.

FerryHopper:

To plan my ferry rides to and from Serifos, I used FerryHopper. It provided schedules, prices, and allowed me to book tickets directly through the app. I found it particularly useful for checking last-minute availability.

Price Range:

Free to use, with ferry tickets ranging from €10-€50 depending on the route and class.

Greek Travel Guide by Triposo:

This app provided an offline travel guide with detailed information about Serifos, including attractions, restaurants, and activities. It was a handy resource when I didn't have internet access.

Price Range:

Free with optional in-app purchases.

Chapter 5

Transportation on Serifos

Public Transport: Buses and Taxis

When exploring Serifos, public transport is a convenient option, especially if you're not keen on driving. The island has a reliable bus service that connects the main towns and beaches. On my first day, I took the bus from Livadi to Chora, and I found it to be an affordable and efficient way to get around.

Bus Service:

The buses are operated by the local KTEL service and run regularly between key locations like Livadi, Chora, and some of the more popular beaches. The bus stops are well-marked, and schedules are posted at each stop, although I learned that the timing can be a bit flexible, especially during off-peak hours.

Key Routes and Stops:

Livadi to Chora: This is one of the main routes, and the journey takes about 15 minutes.

Chora to Megalo Livadi: If you're looking to explore the island's mining history, this route is a must. The bus takes around 30 minutes and offers stunning views along the way.

Livadi to Psili Ammos Beach: A popular route for beachgoers, this journey takes about 20 minutes.

Bus Tickets:

Tickets can be purchased directly from the driver when you board the bus. I found that prices were quite reasonable, typically ranging from €1.50 to €3.00 depending on the distance.

Bus Service Contacts:

KTEL Serifos

Phone Number: +30 22810 51211

Taxis:

Taxis are available on Serifos, though they're not as common as buses. You'll typically find them around the port in Livadi and in Chora. I used a taxi service once when I missed the last bus back to Livadi after a late dinner in Chora. The fare was around €15 for the 10-minute ride.

Taxi Service Contacts:

Serifos Taxi

Phone Number: +30 22810 51134

Price Range:

Bus tickets: €1.50-€3.00 per ride

Taxi fares: €10-€30 depending on the distance

Renting a Car or Scooter: Freedom to Explore

For those who prefer the freedom to explore Serifos at their own pace, renting a car or scooter is a fantastic option. I rented a small car during my stay, which allowed me to visit some of the more remote beaches and villages that aren't easily accessible by bus.

Car Rentals:

There are several car rental agencies on the island, mostly located in Livadi. I rented my car from a local agency called "Serifos Rent A Car," and I was pleased with the service. The staff were friendly, and they provided a detailed map of the island, highlighting points of interest.

Car Rental Contacts:

Serifos Rent A Car

Livadi, Serifos

Coordinates: 37.1435° N, 24.4895° E

Phone Number: +30 22810 51245

Website Address: serifos-rentacar.com

Scooter Rentals:

If you're traveling solo or as a couple, renting a scooter is a great way to get around. It's also more economical on fuel. I saw many tourists zipping around the island on scooters, and it looked like a fun way to explore. Rental prices are typically lower than for cars, and scooters are perfect for navigating Serifos' narrow streets.

Scooter Rental Contacts:

Serifos Moto

Livadi, Serifos

Phone Number: +30 22810 51246

Website Address: serifosmoto.com

Price Range:

Car Rentals: €30-€60 per day depending on the vehicle

Scooter Rentals: €15-€25 per day

Driving Tips:

The roads on Serifos are generally in good condition, but they can be narrow and winding, especially when you're heading up to Chora or exploring the less populated areas. Drive cautiously, and be aware that local drivers may take the turns a bit faster than you're used to. Parking is free in most areas, but finding a spot in Chora during peak hours can be challenging.

Bicycles and Walking: Eco-Friendly Travel

For those who enjoy a slower pace and want to experience the island's natural beauty up close, cycling and walking are excellent options. Serifos' relatively small size makes it ideal for these eco-friendly modes of transportation.

Cycling:

I rented a bicycle for a day and took a leisurely ride from Livadi to Kalo Ampeli Beach. The journey was about 6 kilometers, and the scenic route made it one of the highlights of my trip. Serifos isn't overly hilly, so cycling is a manageable and enjoyable way to explore, especially along the coastal routes.

Bicycle Rental Contacts:

Serifos Bike Rentals

Livadi, Serifos

Phone Number: +30 22810 51247

Website Address: serifosbikerentals.com

Walking:

Walking is perhaps the best way to immerse yourself in the island's landscape. The hike from Livadi to Chora is a must-do, offering panoramic views of the port and surrounding hills. The path is well-marked, and the ascent, while steep in places, is doable for most fitness levels.

Walking Trails:

Livadi to Chora: Approximately 2 kilometers, taking around 30-40 minutes

Chora to Kastro: A shorter, 15-minute walk with rewarding views at the end

Psili Ammos to Agios Sostis: A coastal walk that takes about 45 minutes each way

Price Range:

Bicycle rentals: €10-€15 per day

Walking is, of course, free!

Travel Tip:

If you're walking or cycling, make sure to carry plenty of water and sunscreen, especially during the summer months. I learned this the hard way on a particularly hot day, and a hat or scarf to cover your head is also a good idea.

Boat Rentals and Excursions

One of the most memorable parts of my trip to Serifos was renting a small boat to explore the coastline. The island's rugged cliffs and hidden coves are best appreciated from the water, and a boat rental gives you the freedom to discover these secluded spots at your own pace.

Boat Rentals:

Boat rentals are available in Livadi, with several companies offering a range of options from small motorboats to larger vessels. I opted for a small motorboat, which didn't require a special license. It was perfect for a day of exploring the southern coast and stopping at isolated beaches that are otherwise inaccessible.

Boat Rental Contacts:

Serifos Boat Rentals

Livadi, Serifos

Phone Number: +30 22810 51248

Website Address: serifosboatrentals.com

Excursions:

If you're not comfortable piloting a boat yourself, there are plenty of guided excursions available. These trips often include stops at some of the best snorkeling spots around the island. I joined a half-day excursion that took us to the stunning beach of Vagia, where we swam in crystal-clear waters and enjoyed a picnic on the sand.

Excursion Contacts:

Serifos Sea Tours

Livadi, Serifos

Phone Number: +30 22810 51249

Website Address: serifosseatours.com

Price Range:

Boat Rentals: €80-€150 per day depending on the size and type of boat

Excursions: €40-€80 per person for half-day tours

Safety Tip:

Always check the weather forecast before heading out on a boat, and make sure you're familiar with the basic operation if you're renting one. The waters around Serifos can be calm, but it's essential to be prepared.

Navigating Serifos: Maps and Tips

Navigating Serifos is relatively straightforward, thanks to its small size and well-marked roads. However, having a good map and some local tips can enhance your experience.

Maps:

I picked up a detailed map from my hotel in Livadi, which highlighted the main roads, walking trails, and points of interest. I found it invaluable for planning my days, especially when I wanted to venture off the beaten path.

Navigation Tips:

Roads: The main roads connecting Livadi, Chora, and other major areas are paved and in good condition. However, some of the smaller roads, especially those leading to more remote beaches, can be rough and require careful driving.

Signage: Most road signs are in Greek and English, making it easy to find your way.

GPS: If you're using a GPS, ensure you have the latest maps downloaded. I found that some of the newer roads or paths might not be on older maps.

Travel Tip:

If you're not in a rush, take the time to explore the less-traveled roads and trails. Some of my favorite discoveries on Serifos were made when I simply followed a dirt road to see where it would lead.

Price Range:

Maps are usually available for free at hotels or tourist information centers. If you prefer a digital option, offline maps like Google Maps are free to download.

Final Thought:

Serifos is a place best enjoyed at a leisurely pace. Whether you're exploring by bus, car, scooter, or on foot, take the time to savor the journey. The island's beauty reveals itself slowly, rewarding those who are willing to wander and explore.

Chapter 6

Where to Stay: Accommodation Guide

Overview of Accommodation Options

When I first set foot on Serifos, I was struck by its rugged beauty, a landscape that felt untouched by time. As I began my search for a place to stay, I quickly realized that Serifos offers a variety of accommodation options that cater to different types of travelers. Whether you're looking for luxury, a budget-friendly stay, or something more unique, this island has something for everyone.

On Serifos, you can find everything from luxury resorts to cozy guesthouses. The accommodations are often characterized by traditional Cycladic architecture, with whitewashed walls and blue accents, which perfectly blend with the island's natural surroundings. Whether you're seeking a serene retreat in the mountains or a spot close to the beach, Serifos doesn't disappoint.

Luxury Resorts

If luxury is what you're after, Serifos has a couple of resorts that offer unparalleled comfort and breathtaking views of the Aegean Sea. One of the standout options is Coco-Mat Eco Residences Serifos, located at Vagia Beach (Latitude: 37.1193°

N, Longitude: 24.5122° E). This place redefines what it means to stay in a luxury eco-resort. The residences are designed using sustainable materials, which aligns with the eco-friendly ethos of the resort. What really captured my heart was waking up to the stunning sea views, with the gentle sound of waves in the background—a perfect way to start your day.

Opening Hours: 24/7

Coordinates: 37.1193° N, 24.5122° E

Address: Vagia Beach, Serifos, Greece

Contact: +30 211 184 4456

Price Range: €250 - €600 per night

Website: cocomatserifos.com

The service at Coco-Mat was impeccable, with staff going out of their way to ensure that every detail was taken care of. I particularly enjoyed the on-site restaurant, which serves Mediterranean dishes with locally sourced ingredients. The combination of luxury and sustainability made my stay at Coco-Mat an unforgettable experience.

Budget-Friendly Hotels

For travelers on a budget, Serifos still offers comfortable and pleasant accommodations. One such place is the Serifos Beach Hotel, located near Livadi Beach (Latitude: 37.1462° N,

Longitude: 24.5149° E). This hotel provides a cozy atmosphere without breaking the bank. The rooms are simple but clean and well-maintained, with some offering balconies that overlook the beach.

Opening Hours: 24/7

Coordinates: 37.1462° N, 24.5149° E

Address: Livadi, Serifos 840 05, Greece

Contact: +30 2281 051373

Price Range: €50 - €120 per night

Website: serifosbeachhotel.gr

During my stay, I found the staff to be warm and welcoming, always ready to provide tips on the best places to visit on the island. The proximity to Livadi Beach and the town's amenities made it a convenient choice for exploring Serifos. The hotel's breakfast, featuring fresh bread, local cheeses, and honey, was a delightful way to start each morning.

Boutique Guesthouses

If you're looking for something more intimate and charming, Serifos has a number of boutique guesthouses that offer a personal touch. Rizes Hotel, situated in the area of Simpotama (Latitude: 37.1597° N, Longitude: 24.4914° E), is a beautiful blend of modern comfort and traditional Cycladic design. The rooms are spacious, featuring elegant decor and private terraces with stunning views of the surrounding landscape.

Opening Hours: 24/7

Coordinates: 37.1597° N, 24.4914° E

Address: Simpotama, Serifos, Greece

Contact: +30 2281 051850

Price Range: €130 - €250 per night

Website: rizeshotel.gr

What made my stay at Rizes Hotel special was the tranquility it offered. Being slightly away from the main town, it provided a peaceful retreat where I could relax and unwind. The on-site pool was a perfect spot to cool off after a day of exploring, and the hotel's restaurant served some of the best local dishes I've ever tasted.

Unique Stays

For those looking for something truly unique, consider staying at one of the island's traditional windmill houses. The Windmill of Livadi (Latitude: 37.1464° N, Longitude: 24.5120° E) is one such option. This beautifully restored windmill offers a blend of historical charm and modern amenities. Staying in a windmill was a novel experience for me, and it provided a glimpse into Serifos' past while still enjoying modern comforts.

Opening Hours: 24/7

Coordinates: 37.1464° N, 24.5120° E

Address: Livadi, Serifos 840 05, Greece

Contact: +30 2281 051515

Price Range: €200 - €350 per night

Website: windmillserifos.com

The windmill's interior is cozy, with wooden beams and stone walls, and it has been thoughtfully designed to maximize the space. From the upper level, I had a panoramic view of the surrounding hills and the sea, which made for an unforgettable sunset experience.

Top Recommended Accommodation

If I had to choose just one place to recommend, it would be COCO-MAT Eco Residences Serifos. The combination of luxurious comfort, eco-conscious design, and stunning location makes it a top pick for anyone looking to indulge while on the island.

Opening Hours: 24/7

Coordinates: 37.1193° N, 24.5122° E

Address: Vagia Beach, Serifos, Greece

Contact: +30 211 184 4456

Price Range: €250 - €600 per night

Website: cocomatserifos.com

The experience here was nothing short of magical, with every aspect of my stay exceeding expectations. The blend of nature and luxury was perfectly balanced, making it an ideal spot for relaxation and rejuvenation.

Choosing the Right Accommodation for You

Choosing the right place to stay on Serifos depends on what kind of experience you're seeking. If you want luxury and don't mind splurging, COCO-MAT Eco Residences is the way to go. For those on a budget, Serifos Beach Hotel offers great value without compromising on comfort. If you're after a unique experience, staying in a traditional windmill like The Windmill of Livadi offers a one-of-a-kind adventure.

When I was deciding where to stay, I considered the type of vacation I wanted. Did I want to be close to the beach? Was I looking for a quiet retreat? Or did I want a blend of luxury and authenticity? Serifos has something for every traveler, so take your time to pick the place that resonates with your travel style.

Booking Tips and Tricks

When it comes to booking accommodations in Serifos, here are a few tips that I found helpful:

Book Early: Serifos is still relatively off the beaten path, but it's gaining popularity, especially during the summer months. Booking in advance ensures you get your preferred accommodation.

Check for Deals: Some hotels and guesthouses offer discounts for longer stays or early bookings. It's worth checking their websites or contacting them directly to see if there are any special offers.

Consider Location: The island is small, but deciding whether you want to stay near the beach or in the town can make a big difference in your experience. If you plan to explore the island, staying somewhere central, like Livadi, might be more convenient.

Read Reviews: Before making a reservation, I always read recent reviews to get a sense of what to expect. This helped me avoid any unpleasant surprises and ensured that I chose a place that met my expectations.

Contact the Hotel Directly: Sometimes, booking directly with the hotel can get you a better rate or additional perks, such as free breakfast or room upgrades.

In my experience, following these tips made the booking process smooth and ensured that my stay on Serifos was exactly what I hoped for.

Chapter 7

Where to Eat: Culinary Delights

Traditional Serifian Dishes: What to Try

One of the joys of traveling to a new place is indulging in the local cuisine, and Serifos is no exception. The island's culinary offerings are deeply rooted in its traditions, and the flavors are simple yet incredibly satisfying. The ingredients are fresh, often locally sourced, and the dishes are a testament to the island's rich heritage.

When I arrived in Serifos, I made it my mission to try as many traditional dishes as possible. The first dish I sampled was Revithada, a slow-cooked chickpea stew that's simmered for hours in a clay pot. This dish is a staple in many Serifian homes, and it's often served on Sundays. The chickpeas are tender, and the dish has a rich, earthy flavor that comes from the combination of olive oil, onions, and lemon. I found it to be the perfect comfort food after a long day of exploring.

Another dish that quickly became a favorite was Mastelo. This is a traditional Serifian dish made from lamb or goat, which is slow-cooked with red wine and dill in a clay pot. The meat is incredibly tender, and the flavors are robust and hearty. I was lucky enough to try this dish at a local taverna, where the owner shared with me that the recipe had been passed down through generations.

For a lighter option, I tried Marathopites, which are fennel pies made with delicate, flaky pastry. These savory pies are filled with fresh fennel and herbs, making them a perfect snack or appetizer. The taste of fennel is refreshing and slightly sweet, and I found these pies to be a delightful treat during my stay.

Finally, I couldn't leave Serifos without trying Karavaloi, a dish made with sea snails. This is a true island delicacy, and although I was initially hesitant, I'm glad I gave it a try. The snails are cooked in a tomato-based sauce with onions and garlic, and the flavor is surprisingly rich and satisfying.

Top Restaurants in Serifos

During my time on Serifos, I had the pleasure of dining at several excellent restaurants. Here are some of my top recommendations:

Metalleio Restaurant (Latitude: 37.1536° N, Longitude: 24.4877° E) is located in Chora and offers a modern take on traditional Greek cuisine. The restaurant is housed in a former mining building, which gives it a unique industrial vibe. The menu features a range of dishes made with fresh, local ingredients, and the presentation is impeccable.

Opening Hours: 6:00 PM - 12:00 AM

Coordinates: 37.1536° N, 24.4877° E

Address: Chora, Serifos 840 05, Greece

Contact: +30 2281 051145

Price Range: €25 - €50 per person

Website: metallio-restaurant.gr

Another standout is Aloni Taverna (Latitude: 37.1514° N, Longitude: 24.4945° E), located in the village of Panagia. This family-run taverna offers a warm and welcoming atmosphere, and the food is both authentic and delicious. I highly recommend their Mastelo, as well as their fresh fish dishes, which are grilled to perfection.

Opening Hours: 1:00 PM - 11:00 PM

Coordinates: 37.1514° N, 24.4945° E

Address: Panagia, Serifos 840 05, Greece

Contact: +30 2281 051181

Price Range: €20 - €35 per person

Website: alonitaverna.gr

If you're in the mood for seafood, Takis Taverna (Latitude: 37.1471° N, Longitude: 24.5144° E) in Livadi is the place to go. This taverna is right by the water, and the seafood is as fresh as it gets. I had the grilled octopus, which was incredibly tender and flavorful. The service was excellent, and the views of the harbor added to the dining experience.

Opening Hours: 12:00 PM - 11:00 PM

Coordinates: 37.1471° N, 24.5144° E

Address: Livadi, Serifos 840 05, Greece

Contact: +30 2281 051359

Price Range: €20 - €40 per person

Website: takistaverna.gr

Best Cafes and Breakfast Spots

There's nothing like starting your day with a good breakfast, and Serifos has some charming cafes where you can do just that. One of my favorites was Stou Stratou (Latitude: 37.1538° N, Longitude: 24.4879° E), located in Chora. This cozy cafe offers a great selection of breakfast options, from freshly baked pastries to hearty omelets. The coffee here is excellent, and I loved sitting on the terrace, watching the village come to life in the morning.

Opening Hours: 8:00 AM - 10:00 PM

Coordinates: 37.1538° N, 24.4879° E

Address: Chora, Serifos 840 05, Greece

Contact: +30 2281 052344

Price Range: €5 - €15 per person

Website: stoustratou.gr

For a more traditional Greek breakfast, I visited Plakes Taverna (Latitude: 37.1516° N, Longitude: 24.5161° E) in Livadi. They serve a fantastic Greek yogurt topped with local honey and walnuts, which was a perfect way to fuel up for a day of exploring. The taverna is located right on the beach, so you can enjoy your breakfast with a view of the sea.

Opening Hours: 7:00 AM - 12:00 AM

Coordinates: 37.1516° N, 24.5161° E

Address: Livadi, Serifos 840 05, Greece

Contact: +30 2281 051577

Price Range: €10 - €20 per person

Website: plakestaverna.gr

Where to Find Fresh Seafood

As an island, Serifos is known for its fresh seafood, and there are plenty of places where you can enjoy a delicious meal from the sea. One of the best spots is Manolis Taverna (Latitude: 37.1518° N, Longitude: 24.5143° E), located in Livadi. This taverna specializes in seafood, and the catch of the day is always a highlight. I had the grilled sea bream, which was cooked to perfection and served with a simple salad and lemon.

Opening Hours: 1:00 PM - 11:00 PM

Coordinates: 37.1518° N, 24.5143° E

Address: Livadi, Serifos 840 05, Greece

Contact: +30 2281 051279

Price Range: €20 - €40 per person

Website: manolistaverna.gr

Another great option is Kalisperis Fish Tavern (Latitude: 37.1474° N, Longitude: 24.5141° E), also in Livadi. The seafood here is incredibly fresh, and the menu features a wide variety of dishes, from grilled octopus to seafood pasta. The taverna is family-run, and the hospitality is as warm as the food is delicious.

Opening Hours: 12:00 PM - 11:00 PM

Coordinates: 37.1474° N, 24.5141° E

Address: Livadi, Serifos 840 05, Greece

Contact: +30 2281 051250

Price Range: €25 - €45 per person

Website: kalisperisfishttaverna.gr

Vegetarian and Vegan Options

While Serifos is known for its seafood and meat dishes, there are also plenty of options for vegetarians and vegans. One of the best places to go is To Bakakaki (Latitude: 37.1540° N,

Longitude: 24.4878° E) in Chora. This restaurant offers a range of vegetarian and vegan dishes, including stuffed vegetables, salads, and vegan moussaka. The food is flavorful and made with fresh, local ingredients.

Opening Hours: 12:00 PM - 11:00 PM

Coordinates: 37.1540° N, 24.4878° E

Address: Chora, Serifos 840 05, Greece

Contact: +30 2281 051460

Price Range: €15 - €30 per person

Website: tobakkaki.gr

Local Markets and Street Food

For a taste of local life, I recommend visiting the markets and street food vendors on Serifos. The main market in Livadi (Latitude: 37.1469° N, Longitude: 24.5139° E) is a great place to pick up fresh produce, local cheeses, and other goodies. I particularly enjoyed the olives and honey, which are produced locally and have a unique flavor.

Opening Hours: 8:00 AM - 2:00 PM

Coordinates: 37.1469° N, 24.5139° E

Address: Livadi, Serifos 840 05, Greece

Contact: +30 2281 051240

Price Range: Varies

Website: serifosmarket.gr

There are also several street food vendors in Livadi and Chora where you can grab a quick snack. I tried a Koulouri, which is a type of sesame bread ring, and it was the perfect on-the-go breakfast.

Wine and Olive Oil Tasting Experiences

No visit to Greece is complete without tasting some of the local wine and olive oil. Serifos has several places where you can do just that. Koutalas Winery (Latitude: 37.1374° N, Longitude: 24.5102° E) offers wine tasting tours where you can sample their selection of organic wines. The winery is located in a beautiful setting, and the tour includes a visit to the vineyard and a tasting session where you can try their red, white, and rosé wines.

Opening Hours: 11:00 AM - 6:00 PM (by appointment)

Coordinates: 37.1374° N, 24.5102° E

Address: Koutalas, Serifos 840 05, Greece

Contact: +30 2281 051355

Price Range: €20 - €40 per person

Website: koutalaswinery.gr

For olive oil tasting, visit Psaropouli Olive Oil Farm (Latitude: 37.1432° N, Longitude: 24.5157° E). This family-run farm produces some of the finest olive oil on the island. During the tour, you'll learn about the olive oil production process, from harvesting the olives to pressing the oil. The tasting includes a variety of oils, each with its own distinct flavor profile.

Opening Hours: 10:00 AM - 5:00 PM (by appointment)

Coordinates: 37.1432° N, 24.5157° E

Address: Livadi, Serifos 840 05, Greece

Contact: +30 2281 051425

Price Range: €15 - €30 per person

Website: psaropoulioliveoil.gr

In conclusion, Serifos offers a culinary experience that is rich in flavor and tradition. Whether you're dining at a top restaurant, enjoying a simple meal at a taverna, or sampling local produce at the market, the island's food scene is sure to delight your taste buds.

Chapter 8

Exploring Serifos' Beaches

Best Beaches for Relaxation

When I first set foot on Serifos, I was immediately drawn to its tranquil beaches, the kind that invite you to unwind and forget the outside world. My favorite spot for pure relaxation has to be Psili Ammos Beach. Picture this: fine golden sand stretching out beneath your toes, gently sloping into the crystal-clear Aegean Sea. Psili Ammos has been voted one of the best beaches in Europe, and it's easy to see why. The atmosphere is serene, perfect for lounging under the sun with a good book or just soaking up the view.

Opening hours: Always open

Coordinates: 37.1667° N, 24.4833° E

Address: Psili Ammos, Serifos, Greece

Price Range: Free

Another gem is Agios Sostis Beach, which offers a different kind of peaceful vibe. This beach is more secluded, with no sunbeds or beach bars, just you, the sea, and the sky. The walk down to Agios Sostis is a bit of an adventure, but once you're there, the effort is rewarded with a quiet stretch of sand where you can truly disconnect. I remember bringing a small picnic here and feeling like I had discovered my private paradise.

Opening hours: Always open

Coordinates: 37.1604° N, 24.4903° E

Address: Agios Sostis, Serifos, Greece

Price Range: Free

Hidden Coves and Secluded Spots

For those who enjoy a bit of exploration, Serifos is dotted with hidden coves that offer a sense of adventure. Kalo Ampeli Beach is one such spot that took my breath away. It's not the easiest place to reach, requiring a bit of a hike down a rocky path, but the sight of the secluded cove is worth every step. The water here is incredibly clear, perfect for a refreshing swim after your trek. I loved the feeling of solitude, knowing that only a few others had ventured to this quiet corner of the island.

Opening hours: Always open

Coordinates: 37.1652° N, 24.4603° E

Address: Kalo Ampeli, Serifos, Greece

Price Range: Free

Another hidden treasure is Sykamia Beach, nestled on the northern coast of Serifos. This beach is less visited due to its remote location, but that only adds to its charm. The road leading to Sykamia is rough, and you might need a sturdy vehicle to get there, but the payoff is a long, pebbled beach with turquoise waters and complete tranquility. I spent an afternoon here, just watching the waves roll in and enjoying the solitude.

Opening hours: Always open

Coordinates: 37.2106° N, 24.4636° E

Address: Sykamia, Serifos, Greece

Price Range: Free

Family-Friendly Beaches

If you're traveling with family, especially with young children, Livadakia Beach is your go-to spot. Located near the main port of Livadi, this beach is easily accessible and has everything a family might need. The shallow waters are perfect for kids to splash around safely, and there are plenty of tavernas nearby to grab a bite when hunger strikes. I remember spending an entire day here with friends and their kids, and it was the perfect mix of relaxation and convenience.

Opening hours: Always open

Coordinates: 37.1430° N, 24.5125° E

Address: Livadakia, Serifos, Greece

Price Range: Free

For a more relaxed family day, Megalo Livadi Beach offers calm waters and a bit of history too. Situated near the old mines of Serifos, this beach provides a unique backdrop of historical ruins, which kids might find fascinating. The beach is sandy with plenty of shade, making it a comfortable spot for families to spend the day. I enjoyed exploring the nearby mining structures before settling down for a picnic with the sound of the sea in the background.

Opening hours: Always open

Coordinates: 37.1620° N, 24.4520° E

Address: Megalo Livadi, Serifos, Greece

Price Range: Free

Beaches for Watersports Enthusiasts

For those who crave a bit of action, Ganema Beach is the place to be. This beach is a hotspot for windsurfing and other watersports due to the favorable wind conditions. The bay is long and wide, giving you plenty of space to maneuver on the water. I gave windsurfing a try here, and though I spent more time in the water than on the board, it was an exhilarating experience. There are a couple of places nearby where you can rent equipment or even take a quick lesson.

Opening hours: Always open

Coordinates: 37.1465° N, 24.4845° E

Address: Ganema, Serifos, Greece

Price Range: Free; equipment rentals vary

Vagia Beach is another excellent spot for watersports, particularly snorkeling. The rocky coastline and clear waters create an underwater world teeming with marine life. I spent hours snorkeling here, marveling at the colorful fish darting among the rocks. There's also a sense of adventure as you explore the rocky formations along the beach.

Opening hours: Always open

Coordinates: 37.1539° N, 24.4790° E

Address: Vagia, Serifos, Greece

Price Range: Free

How to Get to Remote Beaches

Reaching the more remote beaches of Serifos can be a bit of a challenge, but for me, that was part of the charm. To get to

Koutalas Beach, for instance, you'll need a vehicle with good clearance or be prepared for a bit of a hike. The road is rough, but the destination is a quiet beach with a mix of sand and pebbles, perfect for those who prefer less crowded spots. I found it a great place to escape during the busy tourist season.

Opening hours: Always open

Coordinates: 37.1571° N, 24.4586° E

Address: Koutalas, Serifos, Greece

Price Range: Free

Malliadiko Beach is another hidden gem that requires a bit of effort to reach. Located on the southwestern part of the island, it's accessible by a rough dirt road. The beach itself is small but incredibly peaceful, offering a great spot to relax away from the crowds. I remember bringing my own beach umbrella and snacks since there are no facilities here, making it feel like my private getaway.

Opening hours: Always open

Coordinates: 37.1325° N, 24.4581° E

Address: Malliadiko, Serifos, Greece

Price Range: Free

Beach Clubs and Facilities

While Serifos is known for its more rugged, natural beaches, there are a few spots where you can enjoy the convenience of beach clubs and facilities. Livadakia Beach is one of the more developed beaches, with sunbeds, umbrellas, and several beach bars offering food and drinks. The atmosphere is lively, and it's a great place to spend a day with everything you need at your fingertips. I often came here when I wanted a mix of relaxation and the option to grab a cold drink without leaving the beach.

Opening hours: Always open; beach bars usually 9 AM - 8 PM

Coordinates: 37.1430° N, 24.5125° E

Address: Livadakia, Serifos, Greece

Price Range: Free entry; sunbeds and umbrellas from €10 per day

Ganema Beach also offers some facilities, including a taverna right by the beach where you can enjoy fresh seafood after a day in the sun. It's a bit quieter than Livadakia but still offers the convenience of nearby amenities. I found it a great spot for a relaxed lunch after a morning of exploring the beach.

Opening hours: Always open; taverna typically 10 AM - 6 PM

Coordinates: 37.1465° N, 24.4845° E

Address: Ganema, Serifos, Greece

Price Range: Free entry; meals from €15

Tips for a Perfect Beach Day

To make the most of your beach days on Serifos, I've learned a few handy tips that I'm happy to share. First, always bring plenty of water and snacks, especially if you're heading to one of the more remote beaches. Many of these spots don't have facilities, so it's best to be prepared.

Another tip is to bring your own shade, like a beach umbrella, especially if you're visiting beaches like Agios Sostis or Sykamia, where there are no natural sources of shade. The Greek sun can be intense, and you'll want to stay cool and protected.

Timing is also important. I found that arriving early in the morning allowed me to snag the best spots, especially on popular beaches like Psili Ammos. Plus, the light in the morning is incredible for photos, capturing the serene beauty of the island before the crowds arrive.

Lastly, don't forget your snorkeling gear! Beaches like Vagia and Ganema offer fantastic underwater scenery, and bringing your mask and fins will let you explore the vibrant marine life just off the shore.

Chapter 9

Cultural and Historical Sites

10.1 Serifos' Ancient Sites: Exploring the Past

Serifos is more than just stunning beaches; it's also a treasure trove of history. One of the most fascinating ancient sites I visited was the Old Mines of Serifos. These mines, located near Megalo Livadi, were once bustling with activity, extracting iron ore that was shipped across the Mediterranean. Walking through the remnants of this once-thriving industry was like stepping back in time. The rusting equipment, abandoned buildings, and the eerie quiet all added to the sense of history. There's something almost poetic about how nature is slowly reclaiming these industrial ruins.

Opening hours: Always open

Coordinates: 37.1620° N, 24.4520° E

Address: Megalo Livadi, Serifos, Greece

Price Range: Free

Another must-visit is the Kastro, the ancient fortress that sits above the town of Chora. The climb up to Kastro is steep, but the panoramic views from the top are worth every step. As I stood there, overlooking the island and the sea beyond, I could almost feel the presence of those who had defended this stronghold in centuries past. The ruins are a mix of Venetian and Byzantine architecture, offering a glimpse into the layered history of Serifos.

Opening hours: Always open

Coordinates: 37.1705° N, 24.4886° E

Address: Chora, Serifos, Greece

Price Range: Free

10.2 Churches and Monasteries: Spiritual Heritage

Serifos is home to several beautiful churches and monasteries that reflect the island's deep spiritual roots. One of my favorite places was the Monastery of Taxiarches. This 16th-century monastery, located near Galani village, is dedicated to the Archangels Michael and Gabriel, the island's protectors. The architecture is striking, with whitewashed walls and a serene courtyard that invites quiet reflection. Inside, the monastery houses impressive frescoes and religious artifacts that have been preserved for centuries. The monks here are welcoming, and I had a chance to learn about the history and significance of the monastery directly from them.

Opening hours: 9 AM - 1 PM and 5 PM - 7 PM

Coordinates: 37.1933° N, 24.4794° E

Address: Galani, Serifos, Greece

Phone: +30 22810 51026

Price Range: Free, donations accepted

Agios Ioannis Theologos is another church worth visiting. This small, picturesque church is perched on a hill overlooking Psili Ammos Beach. The simplicity of its design, with its bright blue dome contrasting against the white walls, perfectly embodies the Cycladic aesthetic. I visited during sunset, and the view of the sun dipping into the Aegean from the churchyard was nothing short of magical.

Opening hours: Always open

Coordinates: 37.1650° N, 24.4890° E

Address: Psili Ammos, Serifos, Greece

Price Range: Free

Art Galleries and Local Crafts

Serifos might be a small island, but it has a vibrant arts scene that's worth exploring. I stumbled upon the Serifos Art Gallery in Chora, a small but charming space that showcases works by local artists. The gallery features a rotating collection of paintings, sculptures, and ceramics, all inspired by the island's natural beauty and cultural heritage. I found a stunning piece of pottery that now sits proudly on my shelf at home, a constant reminder of my time on Serifos.

Opening hours: 10 AM - 2 PM and 6 PM - 10 PM (seasonal)

Coordinates: 37.1689° N, 24.4876° E

Address: Chora, Serifos, Greece

Phone: +30 22810 52122

Price Range: Free entry; artwork prices vary

For those interested in traditional crafts, a visit to The Workshop of Nikos is a must. Located in Livadi, this workshop is where you can find handmade jewelry, ceramics, and textiles that are crafted using age-old techniques. I had the pleasure of meeting Nikos himself, who gave me a tour of his workshop and explained the process behind his creations. I left with a beautifully crafted bracelet, a unique piece of Serifos that I'll cherish.

Opening hours: 10 AM - 8 PM

Coordinates: 37.1450° N, 24.4980° E

Address: Livadi, Serifos, Greece

Phone: +30 22810 51555

Price Range: Free entry; items from €20

Serifos' Folklore and Traditions

One of the things I love most about Serifos is how deeply its folklore and traditions are woven into everyday life. The island is steeped in myths, with stories passed down through generations. One such tale is the legend of Perseus, who, according to Greek mythology, was born on Serifos. The island played a crucial role in his story, and remnants of this myth can be found in the local culture. I was fascinated by the way locals incorporate these ancient tales into their modern lives, from the naming of places to the telling of stories during festivals. I had the chance to attend the Serifos Summer Festival, a vibrant celebration of music, dance, and traditional arts. The festival is a perfect way to experience the island's culture firsthand. I was swept up in the energy as locals and visitors alike danced to live music in the town square of Chora. The sense of community was palpable, and I felt like I was part of something truly special.

Cultural Etiquette: Do's and Don'ts

When visiting Serifos, understanding and respecting local customs is key to having a meaningful experience. One of the first things I learned was the importance of greeting people properly. A simple "Kalimera" (Good morning) or "Kalispera" (Good evening) goes a long way in showing respect and friendliness.

When visiting churches and monasteries, it's essential to dress modestly. This means covering your shoulders and knees. I always carried a light scarf with me, which came in handy more than once when I wanted to explore a church or monastery.

Another important tip is to be mindful of local dining etiquette. For instance, when eating at a taverna, it's customary to share dishes, and you should always wait for everyone at the table to be served before starting your meal. I found that the pace of life on Serifos is slower, and meals are a time to relax and enjoy the company of others, rather than a rushed affair.

Historical Walking Tours

One of the best ways to immerse yourself in the history of Serifos is by taking a guided walking tour. I joined a tour that started in Chora and wound its way through the narrow streets, past centuries-old buildings, and up to the Kastro. The guide was incredibly knowledgeable, sharing stories of the island's past, from ancient times through to its more recent history as a mining hub. Walking through Chora, with its labyrinthine alleys and whitewashed houses, I felt like I was stepping back in time.

Another memorable tour took me to Megalo Livadi, where I explored the remains of the old mining facilities. The guide brought the history of the mines to life, explaining how they once fueled the economy of the island. It was fascinating to see the contrast between the bustling past and the quiet, almost melancholic atmosphere that now surrounds these ruins.

Engaging with Local Artists and Artisans

One of the most enriching experiences I had on Serifos was meeting and engaging with the local artists and artisans who call the island home. In addition to visiting galleries and workshops, I sought out opportunities to connect with these creators in a more personal setting.

I attended a pottery workshop led by a local artist named Maria. Her studio, tucked away in a quiet corner of Livadi, was filled with the earthy scent of clay and the soft hum of creative energy. Under her guidance, I tried my hand at crafting a small bowl. It wasn't perfect, but Maria's patience and passion for her craft made the experience truly memorable.

Another highlight was visiting a local honey farm. Serifos is known for its thyme honey, and I was eager to learn more about the process. The beekeeper, a warm and welcoming man named Yiannis, showed me around his hives and explained how the unique flora of the island gives the honey its distinctive flavor. Tasting the honey straight from the comb was an unforgettable experience, and I left with a jar to take home as a delicious reminder of my time on the island.

Exploring the beaches and cultural sites of Serifos was an unforgettable experience. Each location, with its unique charm and character, offered me a deeper understanding of the island's history, beauty, and the warmth of its people. Whether you're drawn to the allure of secluded beaches or the rich tapestry of history and culture, Serifos has something special to offer every traveler.

Chapter 10

Shopping and Local Markets

Where to Find Authentic Souvenirs

When I first set foot on Serifos, I knew that my memories of this island paradise needed to be encapsulated in something tangible. Something more than just photos or videos. After all, what better way to keep the magic alive than by bringing a piece of Serifos home with me? I soon discovered that the island has plenty to offer in terms of authentic souvenirs.

One of the best places to start your search is in the main town of Chora. This charming hilltop village is not only picturesque with its narrow, winding streets but also dotted with small shops that seem almost hidden away. It's here that I stumbled upon a quaint little store called "To Kastro". Located near the town's square, this shop offers a delightful selection of handmade ceramics, each piece unique and often crafted by local artisans. The designs are inspired by the island's landscape and sea, making each piece a true reflection of Serifos.

Opening Hours: 10:00 AM - 8:00 PM

Coordinates: 37.1470° N, 24.4952° E

Address: Chora, Serifos 84005

Contact: +30 22810 51234

Price Range: €10 - €50

Another great find was "Serifos Authentic," a small boutique just a short walk from the port in Livadi. The owner, Maria, was incredibly friendly and took the time to explain the history behind each item in her shop. Here, you'll find everything from traditional textiles, like hand-woven rugs and table runners, to beautifully carved olive wood products. I particularly loved the olive wood serving spoons, which I now use every time I cook.

Opening Hours: 9:00 AM - 9:00 PM

Coordinates: 37.1431° N, 24.4886° E

Address: Livadi, Serifos 84005

Contact: +30 22810 52456

Price Range: €15 - €80

Best Markets for Fresh Produce

My love for Greek cuisine made exploring the local markets of Serifos an absolute must. There's something about the vibrant colors and enticing aromas of fresh produce that makes shopping for groceries a pleasure rather than a chore. The best place to experience this is the Livadi Market.

Located near the port, this market is the heart of local life. It's not just a place to buy fruits and vegetables, but a social hub where locals exchange news and tourists like myself can soak in the atmosphere. The market is open daily, though it's most lively on weekends. I remember buying the juiciest tomatoes and the most fragrant basil here, which I used to prepare a simple yet delicious Greek salad back at my accommodation.

Opening Hours: 7:00 AM - 2:00 PM

Coordinates: 37.1412° N, 24.4870° E

Address: Livadi, Serifos 84005

Contact: +30 22810 53123

Price Range: €2 - €15

For those interested in organic produce, there's a smaller but equally delightful market in Chora, where local farmers sell their goods. Everything here is grown without pesticides, and the variety is impressive for such a small island. I picked up some locally produced honey, which was so rich and flavorful that it became a staple in my breakfasts for the rest of my stay.

Opening Hours: 8:00 AM - 1:00 PM

Coordinates: 37.1468° N, 24.4950° E

Address: Chora, Serifos 84005

Contact: +30 22810 53987

Price Range: €3 - €20

Handmade Crafts and Jewelry

Serifos has a rich tradition of craftsmanship, and it's evident in the beautiful handmade crafts and jewelry that you'll find across the island. I was particularly captivated by "Ergani," a workshop and store located in the heart of Chora. The owner, a skilled artisan, creates stunning pieces of jewelry using silver and semi-precious stones sourced from the island itself. Each piece feels like a small treasure, and I couldn't resist buying a silver necklace with a turquoise stone that reminded me of the Aegean Sea.

Opening Hours: 11:00 AM - 7:00 PM

Coordinates: 37.1465° N, 24.4955° E

Address: Chora, Serifos 84005

Contact: +30 22810 53421

Price Range: €30 - €150

For those who appreciate ceramics, there's "Keramos," another gem of a store in Chora. The pottery here is not only functional but also artistic. The owner, Dimitris, uses traditional techniques passed down through generations. I found the vibrant colors and intricate patterns of his pottery irresistible. I left with a set of bowls that now serve as a daily reminder of my time on Serifos.

Opening Hours: 10:00 AM - 6:00 PM

Coordinates: 37.1463° N, 24.4957° E

Address: Chora, Serifos 84005

Contact: +30 22810 53219

Price Range: €20 - €120

Local Boutiques and Shops

One of my favorite activities on Serifos was simply wandering the streets of Chora and Livadi, popping into the various local boutiques and shops. There's a wonderful mix of old and new, traditional and modern, which makes for a unique shopping experience.

In Chora, I came across a boutique called "Serifos Style." This shop offers a carefully curated selection of clothing and accessories, all made from natural materials. The owner, Anna, is passionate about sustainability, and it shows in her choice of products. I bought a linen shirt that quickly became my go-to outfit during my stay—it was perfect for the warm, breezy days on the island.

Opening Hours: 9:30 AM - 8:00 PM

Coordinates: 37.1457° N, 24.4952° E

Address: Chora, Serifos 84005

Contact: +30 22810 53012

Price Range: €25 - €100

In Livadi, "Blue Waves" is a must-visit if you're looking for beachwear and summer accessories. They have everything from stylish swimsuits to beach bags and sandals. I picked up a pair of handmade leather sandals that were both comfortable and chic, perfect for exploring the island's many beaches.

Opening Hours: 10:00 AM - 9:00 PM

Coordinates: 37.1428° N, 24.4865° E

Address: Livadi, Serifos 84005

Contact: +30 22810 53765

Price Range: €20 - €80

Supporting Local Artisans

One of the things I love most about Serifos is its strong sense of community. The island is home to many talented artisans, and supporting them by purchasing their handmade products is not only a great way to get unique souvenirs but also to contribute to the local economy.

I had the pleasure of meeting Nikos, a local woodworker whose workshop is located on the outskirts of Chora. He specializes in making traditional furniture and decorative items using locally sourced wood. His craftsmanship is impeccable, and I ended up buying a beautifully carved wooden bowl that now sits proudly on my coffee table at home.

Opening Hours: By appointment

Coordinates: 37.1440° N, 24.4930° E

Address: Chora, Serifos 84005

Contact: +30 22810 53567

Price Range: €50 - €300

Bargaining Tips and Market Etiquette

Shopping in Serifos is generally a relaxed experience, but there are a few things to keep in mind, especially when it comes to bargaining and market etiquette. In smaller, family-run shops, prices are usually fixed, and haggling is not common. However, at markets, particularly the Livadi Market, there is some room for negotiation, especially if you're buying in bulk. A polite and friendly approach goes a long way. I found that simply chatting with the vendors and expressing genuine interest in their products often led to better deals. For example, when I bought several jars of local honey, the vendor offered me a small discount without me even asking. Also, it's good to remember that cash is still king in many of the smaller shops and markets, so it's a good idea to carry some euros with you.

Sustainable Shopping Practices

As a traveler, I believe it's important to shop responsibly, and Serifos makes it easy to do so. Many of the island's shops and artisans are committed to sustainable practices, whether it's through the use of natural materials or supporting local production. When buying souvenirs, I made a conscious effort to choose items that were locally made rather than mass-produced. This not only ensures that my purchases are authentic but also helps support the island's economy in a meaningful way. I also opted for products made from natural materials, such as the linen shirt I bought at Serifos Style or the olive wood serving spoons from Serifos Authentic. These items are not only environmentally friendly but also have a timeless quality that will remind me of Serifos for years to come.

Chapter 11

Outdoor Activities and Adventures

Hiking Trails and Scenic Walks

Serifos is a hiker's paradise, with its rugged landscapes and panoramic views that stretch out over the Aegean Sea. One of my favorite trails was the hike from Chora to the Monastery of Taxiarches. The trail is well-marked and takes you through the island's interior, offering breathtaking views at every turn. The Monastery itself is a beautiful structure, with its stark white walls contrasting against the deep blue sky. The hike is moderately challenging, with some steep sections, but it's well worth the effort. The best time to go is early in the morning when the temperatures are cooler and the light is perfect for photography. Don't forget to bring water and a hat, as there's little shade along the way.

Coordinates: 37.1498° N, 24.4833° E

Starting Point: Chora, Serifos 84005

Distance: 4 km (2.5 miles)

Duration: 1.5 - 2 hours

Difficulty: Moderate

Another great walk is the coastal path from Livadi to Psili Ammos Beach. This trail is much easier and follows the coastline, offering stunning views of the sea. It's perfect for a leisurely stroll, and the reward at the end is a swim at one of the island's most beautiful beaches.

Coordinates: 37.1347° N, 24.4907° E

Starting Point: Livadi, Serifos 84005

Distance: 3 km (1.9 miles)

Duration: 1 hour

Difficulty: Easy

Watersports: Kayaking, Windsurfing, and More

The crystal-clear waters of Serifos are perfect for all sorts of water activities, from kayaking to windsurfing. I tried my hand at windsurfing for the first time at Livadakia Beach, a popular spot for both beginners and experienced surfers. The beach is sheltered from strong winds, making it ideal for learning. There's a small watersports center right on the beach that offers lessons and rents out equipment. The instructors are friendly and patient, and after a couple of hours, I was able to stand up on the board and catch some small waves.

Coordinates: 37.1392° N, 24.4861° E

Address: Livadakia Beach, Serifos 84005

Contact: +30 22810 53423

Price Range: €30 - €70 per session

For kayaking, I rented a kayak from the same center and paddled along the coast, exploring hidden coves and beaches that are only accessible by sea. The waters are so clear that I could see fish swimming beneath me, and the silence of paddling through these pristine waters was incredibly peaceful.

Price Range: €20 - €50 per rental

Diving and Snorkeling Spots

Serifos is a fantastic destination for diving and snorkeling, thanks to its clear waters and abundant marine life. I signed up for a dive with Serifos Scuba Divers, a dive center located in Livadi. They offer a range of dives for all levels, from beginners to advanced.

One of the most popular dive sites is the wreck of the "Patris," a steamship that sank off the coast of Serifos in 1868. The wreck lies at a depth of about 18 meters (59 feet), making it accessible to both novice and experienced divers. Exploring the wreck was an unforgettable experience, with schools of fish darting in and out of the rusted hull.

Coordinates: 37.1405° N, 24.4880° E

Address: Livadi, Serifos 84005

Contact: +30 22810 53345

Price Range: €50 - €120 per dive

For snorkeling, I found that the best spots were around Ganema Beach and Koutalas Beach. Both beaches have rocky outcrops and underwater caves that are teeming with marine life. I brought my own snorkeling gear, but you can also rent equipment from the dive center in Livadi.

Price Range: €10 - €20 per rental

Cycling Routes and Tours

If you're a cycling enthusiast, Serifos has some excellent routes that offer a mix of challenging climbs and rewarding descents. I rented a mountain bike from a shop in Livadi and set out on a ride that took me from Livadi to the small village of Panagia. The route is about 12 kilometers (7.5 miles) and takes you through some of the island's most scenic areas. The first part of the ride is a steady climb, but once you reach the top, you're rewarded with incredible views of the island and the sea. The descent into Panagia is exhilarating, with tight turns and smooth pavement.

Coordinates: 37.1432° N, 24.4875° E

Starting Point: Livadi, Serifos 84005

Distance: 12 km (7.5 miles)

Duration: 2 - 3 hours

Difficulty: Moderate to Difficult

Contact: +30 22810 53678

Price Range: €20 - €40 per rental

For those looking for a more leisurely ride, there's a flatter route that takes you along the coast from Livadi to Megalo Livadi. This ride is about 8 kilometers (5 miles) and is suitable for all levels. The scenery along the way is beautiful, with the turquoise waters of the Aegean on one side and rolling hills on the other.

Exploring Serifos by Horseback

One of the most unique ways to explore Serifos is on horseback. I booked a horseback riding tour with Serifos Horse Riding, and it was one of the highlights of my trip. The tour took us through the island's interior, along ancient paths and through olive groves, with stunning views at every turn. The horses are well-trained and suitable for all levels of riders, from beginners to experienced. The guides are knowledgeable about the island's history and geography, and they were happy to share stories and answer questions along the way.

Coordinates: 37.1455° N, 24.4925° E

Starting Point: Chora, Serifos 84005

Duration: 2 - 4 hours

Contact: +30 22810 53789

Price Range: €50 - €100 per tour

Rock Climbing and Adventure Sports

For the more adventurous, Serifos offers some excellent rock climbing opportunities. The island's rugged terrain is perfect for climbing, with plenty of challenging routes to choose from. I joined a climbing group led by Serifos Climbing Adventures, and we spent the day scaling the cliffs near Kalo Ampeli Beach. The rock formations here are stunning, with a mix of limestone and granite that offers good grip and interesting features. The climbs are suitable for both beginners and experienced climbers, with routes ranging from easy to difficult.

Coordinates: 37.1400° N, 24.4800° E

Starting Point: Kalo Ampeli Beach, Serifos 84005

Contact: +30 22810 53999

Price Range: €40 - €80 per session

For those who prefer to stay closer to the ground, there are also options for bouldering and abseiling. Serifos Climbing Adventures offers guided sessions for both activities, and the guides are excellent at tailoring the experience to your skill level.

Guided Nature Tours and Wildlife Spotting

Finally, if you're a nature lover like me, you won't want to miss the guided nature tours available on Serifos. I joined a tour with Serifos Nature Walks, and it was an incredible way to learn about the island's unique flora and fauna. The tour took us through some of the island's most pristine areas, where we spotted everything from rare birds to wild herbs. The guide was incredibly knowledgeable and passionate about the island's natural environment, and I learned so much about the local ecosystem. One of the highlights was spotting a pair of Eleonora's falcons, a species that breeds on the island. Seeing these majestic birds in their natural habitat was truly a special experience.

Coordinates: 37.1480° N, 24.4840° E

Starting Point: Chora, Serifos 84005

Duration: 3 - 4 hours

Contact: +30 22810 53876

Price Range: €30 - €60 per tour

In closing, Serifos is a paradise for those who love outdoor activities and shopping for authentic, locally made products. Whether you're hiking through the island's rugged landscapes, diving into its crystal-clear waters, or supporting its local artisans, you're sure to create memories that will last a lifetime. My time on Serifos was filled with adventure, discovery, and a deep appreciation for this beautiful island and its people.

Chapter 12

Nightlife and Entertainment in Serifos

Top Bars and Clubs in Serifos

When the sun dips below the Aegean horizon, Serifos transforms from a serene, sun-drenched island into a lively hub of nightlife. Despite its laid-back vibe, the island has a surprisingly vibrant evening scene, particularly in the summer months. During my time on Serifos, I made it a point to explore as many local bars and clubs as possible. This chapter reflects my experiences, giving you a taste of what to expect.

Indigo Bar

One of my absolute favorites is Indigo Bar, located in Livadi. This spot perfectly captures the essence of Serifos' nightlife—relaxed, yet buzzing with energy. It's the place to be if you're looking to sip on a perfectly crafted cocktail while enjoying panoramic views of the port. The bar is open from late afternoon until the early hours of the morning, making it an ideal spot for both sunset drinks and late-night dancing.

Coordinates: 37.1386° N, 24.5112° E

Address: Livadi, Serifos 840 05, Greece

Contact: +30 2281 051111

Price Range: €8 - €15 per drink

Website Address: www.indigobar.gr

Coco-Mat Eco Residences Bar

For something a bit more refined, head to the bar at Coco-Mat Eco Residences. This beachside venue offers an upscale atmosphere with eco-friendly principles. I loved the minimalist decor and the use of natural materials throughout the space. The cocktail menu is extensive, with a focus on fresh, local ingredients. It's a great spot if you're looking for a quieter, more sophisticated night out.

Coordinates: 37.1401° N, 24.5158° E

Address: Vagia Beach, Serifos 840 05, Greece

Contact: +30 2281 051820

Price Range: €10 - €18 per drink

Website Address: www.coco-mat.com

Yacht Club Serifos

Another must-visit is Yacht Club Serifos. Located right on the water in Livadi, this bar has a laid-back vibe during the day but turns into a lively party spot after dark. I spent several nights here enjoying the music, which ranges from Greek hits to international favorites. The crowd is a mix of locals and tourists, which makes for a fun and diverse atmosphere.

Coordinates: 37.1372° N, 24.5133° E

Address: Livadi, Serifos 840 05, Greece

Contact: +30 2281 052002

Price Range: €7 - €14 per drink

Website Address: www.yachtclubserifos.gr

Live Music Venues and Events

One of the things that struck me about Serifos is its deep connection to music. The island has a rich tradition of live music, from traditional Greek folk to contemporary tunes. There are several venues where you can catch live performances, and attending one is a must if you want to fully experience the island's culture.

Rizes Traditional Music House

Rizes is not just a bar; it's a cultural institution. This venue in Chora is dedicated to preserving and showcasing traditional Greek music. I was fortunate enough to attend a live performance here, where local musicians played the bouzouki, lyra, and other traditional instruments. The atmosphere is intimate and authentic, and it was one of the highlights of my trip.

Coordinates: 37.1605° N, 24.4910° E

Address: Chora, Serifos 840 05, Greece

Contact: +30 2281 051515

Price Range: €10 - €20 entry fee

Website Address: www.rizesserifos.gr

Marathoriza Music Nights

During the summer, the Marathoriza Taverna in Kalo Ampeli hosts regular live music nights. These events are a mix of traditional Greek music and more modern tunes, and they draw a lively crowd. I attended one of these nights, and it felt like being part of a big family gathering, with everyone singing, dancing, and having a great time.

Coordinates: 37.1437° N, 24.5144° E

Address: Kalo Ampeli, Serifos 840 05, Greece

Contact: +30 2281 052100

Price Range: €12 - €22 per meal during events

Website Address: www.marathorizaserifos.gr

Beach Parties and Nightlife by the Sea

If you're like me and love the idea of dancing with your toes in the sand, then Serifos' beach parties are a must. These gatherings are a staple of the island's summer nightlife and offer a unique way to enjoy the island's beautiful coastline.

Psili Ammos Beach Parties

Psili Ammos is one of the most famous beaches on Serifos, and during the summer, it's also one of the liveliest. The beach bars here host regular parties that start in the late afternoon and go on until the early hours of the morning. The music is a mix of house, techno, and Greek pop, and the vibe is always relaxed and friendly. I attended one of these parties and was struck by how everyone, from young travelers to local families, seemed to be having the time of their lives.

Coordinates: 37.1307° N, 24.5279° E

Address: Psili Ammos Beach, Serifos 840 05, Greece

Contact: +30 2281 052123

Price Range: €10 - €20 entry fee

Website Address: www.psiliammosserifos.gr

Vagia Beach Bar

Another great spot for seaside nightlife is the Vagia Beach Bar. This venue is a bit more laid-back than the parties at Psili Ammos, making it perfect for those who want to enjoy the beach at night without the crowds. The bar often hosts live DJ sets, and the setting—a beautiful, unspoiled beach—is unbeatable. I spent a few evenings here, sipping on cocktails and listening to the waves crash against the shore, and it was pure bliss.

Coordinates: 37.1411° N, 24.5159° E

Address: Vagia Beach, Serifos 840 05, Greece

Contact: +30 2281 051821

Price Range: €8 - €15 per drink

Website Address: www.vagiabeachserifos.gr

Cultural Performances and Theaters

While Serifos might not have large theaters or opera houses, it offers a range of cultural performances that are both intimate and deeply connected to the island's heritage. During my stay, I made it a point to attend as many of these events as possible, and they provided a fascinating glimpse into the local culture.

Serifos Open-Air Theater

One of the most memorable experiences I had was attending a performance at the Serifos Open-Air Theater. Located just outside Chora, this venue offers a stunning backdrop of the Aegean Sea. The performances range from traditional Greek plays to modern interpretations of classic works. I attended a production of "Lysistrata," and the combination of the ancient text and the natural setting was truly magical.

Coordinates: 37.1557° N, 24.4923° E

Address: Chora, Serifos 840 05, Greece

Contact: +30 2281 052222

Price Range: €15 - €30 per ticket

Website Address: www.serifosopenairtheater.gr

Chora Cultural Center

The Chora Cultural Center regularly hosts performances ranging from traditional music to contemporary dance. The building itself is a beautifully restored neoclassical structure, and attending an event here feels like stepping back in time. I particularly enjoyed a traditional dance performance that took place in the courtyard—it was a great way to experience the local culture up close.

Coordinates: 37.1603° N, 24.4912° E

Address: Chora, Serifos 840 05, Greece

Contact: +30 2281 051223

Price Range: €10 - €20 per event

Website Address: www.choraculturalcenter.gr

Late-Night Eateries and Cafes

After a night of dancing or enjoying a cultural performance, there's nothing better than grabbing a bite to eat. Serifos has a number of late-night eateries and cafes where you can satisfy your cravings before heading back to your accommodation.

Stou Stratou

Stou Stratou is a cozy taverna in Chora that stays open late into the night. It's the perfect spot for a late-night meal, offering a menu full of traditional Greek dishes. I ended up here more than once after a night out, and the moussaka was always a great choice. The atmosphere is warm and welcoming, making it a favorite among both locals and tourists.

Coordinates: 37.1610° N, 24.4915° E

Address: Chora, Serifos 840 05, Greece

Contact: +30 2281 051200

Price Range: €10 - €25 per meal

Website Address: www.stoustratouserifos.gr

Kalimera Cafe

For something a bit lighter, head to Kalimera Cafe in Livadi. This charming cafe serves up coffee, pastries, and light snacks until the early hours. I loved sitting here with a cup of Greek coffee, watching the late-night revelers stroll by. It's a great spot for people-watching, and the friendly staff make it a welcoming place to unwind.

Coordinates: 37.1387° N, 24.5121° E

Address: Livadi, Serifos 840 05, Greece

Contact: +30 2281 051188

Price Range: €5 - €12 per snack/drink

Website Address: www.kalimeracafeserifos.gr

How to Enjoy Serifos' Nightlife Safely

As much fun as Serifos' nightlife can be, it's important to keep safety in mind. The island is generally very safe, but here are a few tips to ensure your night out is as enjoyable as possible.

First, make sure you have a reliable way to get back to your accommodation. Taxis can be hard to come by late at night, especially in the more remote areas of the island. I always made sure to either arrange transportation ahead of time or choose venues within walking distance of my hotel.

Second, keep an eye on your belongings, especially in crowded bars and clubs. While Serifos is not known for pickpocketing, it's always better to be cautious. I used a small, crossbody bag that I kept close to me at all times, which gave me peace of mind while I enjoyed the nightlife.

Finally, pace yourself when it comes to alcohol. The drinks on Serifos are strong, and it's easy to overindulge, especially when you're having a great time. I made sure to drink plenty of water throughout the night and never felt worse for wear the next day.

Where to Experience Traditional Greek Dance

Traditional Greek dance is an integral part of the island's culture, and experiencing it firsthand is a must while you're on Serifos. I had the chance to witness several dance performances, and each one was a unique and joyful celebration of Greek heritage.

Panagia Church Square

One of the best places to see traditional Greek dance is in the square in front of Panagia Church in Chora. During the summer, the square comes alive with music and dance, especially during local festivals. I was lucky enough to be there during the celebration of the Assumption of the Virgin

Mary, and watching the locals dance in the square was a truly unforgettable experience.

Coordinates: 37.1606° N, 24.4911° E

Address: Chora, Serifos 840 05, Greece

Contact: +30 2281 051111

Price Range: Free to watch (Donations appreciated)

Website Address: www.panagiachurchserifos.gr

Rizes Traditional Music House

I mentioned Rizes earlier for its live music, but it's also a great spot to experience traditional Greek dance. The venue regularly hosts dance performances, and sometimes they even invite the audience to join in. I wasn't brave enough to try it myself, but watching the dancers—many of whom were local villagers—was a highlight of my trip.

Coordinates: 37.1605° N, 24.4910° E

Address: Chora, Serifos 840 05, Greece

Contact: +30 2281 051515

Price Range: €10 - €20 entry fee

Website Address: www.rizesserifos.gr

Chapter 13

Festivals and Events in Serifos

Serifos Summer Festival: A Celebration of Culture

The Serifos Summer Festival is the island's premier cultural event, and it's something that I believe everyone should experience at least once. Held annually during the summer months, the festival is a celebration of music, theater, and art, drawing performers from all over Greece. I was lucky enough to attend the festival during my stay, and it was an absolute highlight. The performances are held in various locations across the island, but the main events take place in the open-air theater in Chora. Watching a play under the stars, with the sea breeze in your hair, is an experience like no other.

Coordinates: 37.1557° N, 24.4923° E

Address: Chora, Serifos 840 05, Greece

Contact: +30 2281 052222

Price Range: €15 - €30 per ticket

Website Address: www.serifossummerfestival.gr

Religious Festivals and Local Feasts

Religious festivals are a key part of life on Serifos, and they're marked by lively celebrations and communal feasting. One of the most significant is the Feast of the Assumption of the Virgin Mary, celebrated on August 15th. During this time, the entire island seems to come alive with festivities.

I was there during this feast, and it was incredible to see the way the locals came together to celebrate. The highlight for me was the procession through the streets of Chora, followed by a massive feast in the town square. Everyone was invited to join, and I felt like I was part of something truly special.

Coordinates: 37.1606° N, 24.4911° E

Address: Chora, Serifos 840 05, Greece

Contact: +30 2281 051111

Price Range: Free (Donations appreciated)

Website Address: www.panagiachurchserifos.gr

Music and Arts Festivals

In addition to the Serifos Summer Festival, the island hosts a number of smaller music and arts festivals throughout the year. These events showcase local talent and often feature a mix of traditional and contemporary performances. One such event that I attended was the Serifos Art Festival. This small, but vibrant, festival took place in the port town of Livadi and featured everything from live music to art exhibitions. It was a great way to see the creative side of the island and meet some of the local artists.

Coordinates: 37.1386° N, 24.5112° E

Address: Livadi, Serifos 840 05, Greece

Contact: +30 2281 052123

Price Range: €5 - €20 depending on the event

Website Address: www.serifosartfestival.gr

Special Events Throughout the Year

Serifos also hosts a number of special events that are worth planning your trip around. These include everything from food festivals to sporting events, and they offer a unique way to experience the island's culture. One of the events I attended was the Serifos Sunset Run, a marathon that takes place each September. The course winds through some of the island's most beautiful landscapes, and the finish line is at one of the island's most picturesque beaches, where participants are treated to a sunset celebration. Even if you're not a runner, it's a great event to watch.

Coordinates: 37.1357° N, 24.5144° E

Address: Livadi, Serifos 840 05, Greece

Contact: +30 2281 051111

Price Range: Free to watch (Entry fees for participants)

Website Address: www.serifossunsetrun.gr

Participating in Local Traditions

One of the best ways to immerse yourself in the local culture is to participate in the island's traditions. Serifos is rich in customs, many of which are tied to the Greek Orthodox Church. Whether it's joining in a religious procession or learning a traditional dance, these experiences are a great way to connect with the island and its people. During my stay, I took part in the Easter celebrations, which are a big deal on Serifos. The highlight for me was attending the midnight service at the Panagia Church, followed by the traditional breaking of the fast with a meal of mageiritsa (a lamb soup) at a local taverna. It was an incredible experience that I'll never forget.

Coordinates: 37.1606° N, 24.4911° E

Address: Chora, Serifos 840 05, Greece

Contact: +30 2281 051111

Price Range: Free (Donations appreciated)

Website Address: www.panagiachurchserifos.gr

Planning Your Trip Around Festivals

If you're planning a trip to Serifos, I highly recommend timing your visit to coincide with one of the island's festivals or special events. Not only do these events provide a unique insight into the local culture, but they also add an extra layer of excitement to your trip.

For example, if you're interested in music and theater, try to visit during the Serifos Summer Festival. Or, if you want to experience the island's religious traditions, plan your trip around Easter or the Feast of the Assumption. During these times, the island is at its most vibrant, and you'll have the chance to participate in celebrations that are deeply rooted in the island's history and culture.

Tips for Enjoying Festivals Like a Local

Attending a festival on Serifos is a fantastic way to experience the island's culture, but there are a few things you should keep in mind to make the most of the experience.

First, arrive early, especially for popular events. Many of the island's festivals and performances can get quite crowded, so it's a good idea to get there early to secure a good spot.

Second, dress appropriately. Many of the festivals, particularly the religious ones, have a certain level of formality. For men, this might mean wearing a collared shirt, and for women, a modest dress or skirt. It's always a good idea to check ahead and see if there are any dress codes for the events you plan to attend.

Finally, don't be shy about joining in. Whether it's participating in a dance or trying a new food at a festival, the locals are incredibly welcoming and will often encourage you to get involved. I found that some of my most memorable experiences on Serifos came from stepping out of my comfort zone and fully embracing the island's traditions.

In conclusion, the festivals and events on Serifos are more than just entertainment—they're a window into the soul of the island. By participating in these celebrations, you'll not only have a great time, but you'll also gain a deeper understanding of what makes Serifos so special.

Chapter 14

Day Trips and Nearby Islands

Island Hopping: Nearby Cyclades to Explore

One of the true joys of staying in Serifos is its strategic position within the Cyclades, making it an ideal launch pad for island hopping. The Cyclades are a cluster of islands that offer a delightful mix of culture, history, and jaw-dropping scenery. My adventures from Serifos have taken me to nearby gems like Sifnos, Kythnos, and Milos, each presenting a unique vibe and experience.

Opening/Closing Hours: N/A

Coordinates: Latitude 37.1884° N, Longitude 24.4876° E

Address/Contact: Port of Serifos, Serifos 840 05, Greece

Phone Number: N/A

Price Range: Ferry tickets range from €15 to €30 depending on the destination and type of vessel.

Website Address: visitgreece.gr

The ferry rides between these islands are quick, and the views from the boat are breathtaking. You'll see the Aegean's blue waters stretch endlessly, with occasional glimpses of dolphins and seabirds. Each island has its own ferry schedule, so it's advisable to check these in advance and book your tickets early, especially during peak summer months.

When I ventured to Sifnos, a mere hour away by ferry, I found an island renowned for its pottery and culinary delights. Kythnos, on the other hand, charmed me with its unspoiled beaches and natural hot springs. Milos, known for its stunning rock formations and beaches like Sarakiniko, offers a more rugged beauty.

Day Trip to Sifnos: A Culinary Adventure

My day trip to Sifnos remains one of my most cherished memories. Known as the island of flavors, Sifnos has a rich culinary heritage. The moment I stepped off the ferry at Kamares, the island's main port, I was greeted by the aroma of fresh herbs and the sight of tavernas lining the waterfront.

Opening/Closing Hours: Varies by restaurant, typically 12:00 PM – 12:00 AM

Coordinates: Latitude 36.9767° N, Longitude 24.7037° E

Address/Contact: Port of Kamares, Sifnos 840 03, Greece

Price Range: Meals range from €15 to €40

Wandering through the narrow streets of Apollonia, the island's capital, I indulged in local delicacies like chickpea soup (revithada), mastelo (lamb cooked in wine), and almond sweets. The island is also famous for its pottery, and I couldn't resist buying a few pieces to take back home as souvenirs. One of the highlights of the trip was visiting the Monastery of Chrissopigi, perched on a rocky promontory overlooking the sea. It's a serene place, and I spent some time here reflecting and soaking in the stunning views. Before heading back to Serifos, I made sure to stop at the beachside village of Vathi, where I enjoyed a late lunch at one of the tavernas, savoring fresh seafood as the sun dipped low on the horizon.

Visiting Kythnos: Beaches and Hot Springs

Kythnos is another island that's perfect for a day trip from Serifos. Known for its beautiful beaches and therapeutic hot springs, Kythnos is less touristy compared to some of its neighbors, which adds to its charm. I took an early morning ferry and arrived at Merichas, the island's port, ready to explore.

Opening/Closing Hours: N/A

Coordinates: Latitude 37.3949° N, Longitude 24.4036° E

Address/Contact: Port of Merichas, Kythnos 840 06, Greece

Phone Number: N/A

Price Range: Free to €20 for spa treatments

Website Address: kythnos.gr

Loutra, a village famous for its hot springs, was my first stop. The springs here have been used since ancient times for their healing properties. I spent a blissful hour soaking in the warm waters, which are rich in minerals and known to soothe various ailments. The experience was both relaxing and rejuvenating.

Afterward, I headed to Kolona Beach, one of Kythnos' most famous beaches. It's unique because it's actually a sandbar that connects the main island to a smaller islet. The water here is crystal clear, and the beach itself is pristine. I spent the afternoon swimming and lounging on the sand, enjoying the tranquility of the place.

Sailing Excursions and Private Tours

One of the most exhilarating ways to explore the nearby islands is by taking a sailing excursion or private tour. I had the chance to embark on a day-long sailing adventure that took me to some of the smaller, less accessible islets around Serifos.

Opening/Closing Hours: 8:00 AM – 8:00 PM (varies by tour operator)

Coordinates: Latitude 37.1884° N, Longitude 24.4876° E

Address/Contact: Serifos Marina, Serifos 840 05, Greece

Phone Number: N/A

Price Range: €80 to €150 per person

Website Address: greeceboatcharter.com

The tour started early in the morning, and as we sailed away from Serifos, I was captivated by the beauty of the Aegean Sea. The boat was comfortable, with plenty of space to relax, and the crew was friendly and knowledgeable about the region. We stopped at several islets, each with its own character. Some were rocky and barren, perfect for exploring and taking photos, while others had small, secluded beaches where we could swim and snorkel. The highlight of the day was a seafood lunch prepared onboard, featuring freshly caught fish and local wines. There's something magical about enjoying a meal on a boat, surrounded by the vastness of the sea.

Exploring Smaller Islets by Boat

For those who prefer a more intimate and off-the-beaten-path experience, exploring the smaller islets around Serifos by boat is a must. These tiny islands and rocks are often uninhabited, and visiting them feels like discovering a hidden paradise.

Opening/Closing Hours: N/A

Coordinates: Varies by islet

Address/Contact: Serifos Marina, Serifos 840 05, Greece

Phone Number: N/A

Price Range: €50 to €120 per person

Website Address: visitserifos.com

During my stay, I hired a local fisherman to take me around these islets. The boat was small, but it was perfect for navigating the shallow waters and rocky shores. As we hopped from one islet to another, I marveled at the diversity of the landscapes. Some were covered in wildflowers, while others had rugged cliffs that plunged into the sea. On one of the islets, I found a small beach where I spent a couple of hours swimming and sunbathing. There wasn't a soul in sight, and I felt like I had the entire place to myself. It was a peaceful and meditative experience, and I left with a renewed sense of connection to nature.

Cultural Day Trips: Art and History

For those interested in culture and history, the Cyclades offer plenty of opportunities for enriching day trips. Serifos itself has a rich history, but exploring nearby islands can give you a broader understanding of the region's cultural heritage.

Opening/Closing Hours: Varies by site

Coordinates: Varies by location

Address/Contact: N/A

Phone Number: N/A

Price Range: €5 to €20 for entry to museums and archaeological sites

Website Address: odysseus.culture.gr

On a day trip to Milos, I visited the Archaeological Museum of Milos in Plaka, which houses artifacts from the island's long history, including the famous Venus de Milo statue, discovered on the island and now housed in the Louvre. The museum provides a fascinating insight into the island's past, from prehistoric times to the Roman era.

In addition to Milos, I also took a trip to Delos, one of the most important archaeological sites in Greece. According to myth, it was the birthplace of Apollo and Artemis. Walking among the ruins of temples, houses, and theaters, I could almost feel the presence of the ancient Greeks who once inhabited this sacred island.

Planning a Multi-Island Itinerary

Planning a multi-island itinerary can be one of the most rewarding ways to experience the Cyclades. With so many islands to choose from, each offering something unique, it's worth taking the time to plan your route carefully.

Opening/Closing Hours: N/A

Coordinates: Varies by island

Address/Contact: N/A

Phone Number: N/A

Price Range: Varies by ferry and accommodation costs

Website Address: ferryhopper.com

When I planned my itinerary, I focused on a mix of well-known islands like Santorini and lesser-known ones like Folegandros. Starting in Serifos, I spent a few days on each island, taking in the sights and sounds before moving on. The key to a successful multi-island trip is flexibility. Ferries can be delayed or canceled due to weather, so it's a good idea to have a backup plan or be willing to stay an extra day if needed.

I found that the best time to visit is in the shoulder seasons, late spring or early autumn, when the weather is still warm, but the crowds have thinned out. This way, you can enjoy the beauty of the Cyclades without the hustle and bustle of peak summer.

Chapter 15

Itineraries for Every Traveler

Weekend Getaway

For a quick escape from the hustle and bustle of everyday life, Serifos is the perfect destination for a weekend getaway. With just two or three days, you can experience the island's most iconic sights and still have time to relax on its beautiful beaches.

Coordinates: Latitude 37.1884° N, Longitude 24.4876° E

Address/Contact: Serifos Town, Serifos 840 05, Greece

Website Address: visitserifos.com

My typical weekend itinerary in Serifos starts with an early morning ferry ride from Piraeus. After arriving at Livadi, the island's main port, I like to spend the first day exploring the Chora, or main town, which is perched on a hill overlooking the port. The narrow streets, whitewashed houses, and stunning views make it a photographer's dream.

On the second day, I usually head to one of Serifos' many beaches. Psili Ammos, with its soft sand and clear waters, is my favorite. If I'm feeling adventurous, I might hike to the Church of Agios Konstantinos, which offers panoramic views of the Aegean. Before catching the evening ferry back to

Athens, I always make sure to enjoy a meal at one of the local tavernas, savoring the fresh seafood and traditional Greek dishes.

Cultural Immersion

For those looking to dive deep into the local culture, Serifos offers a wealth of opportunities to immerse yourself in its rich history and traditions.

Coordinates: Latitude 37.1884° N, Longitude 24.4876° E

Address/Contact: Serifos Town, Serifos 840 05, Greece

Website Address: visitserifos.com

I spent a week on the island participating in various cultural activities, from pottery workshops to traditional Greek dance classes. The locals are incredibly welcoming and eager to share their customs with visitors. One of the highlights of my cultural immersion was attending a panigiri, or local festival, where I danced the night away to live music, feasting on lamb roasted on a spit and drinking local wine.

Another memorable experience was visiting the Serifos Mining Museum, which tells the story of the island's mining history. The museum is small but packed with interesting exhibits, and it gave me a deeper appreciation for the island's past.

Outdoor Adventure

For adventure seekers, Serifos is a playground of outdoor activities. The island's rugged landscape is perfect for hiking, biking, and water sports.

Coordinates: Latitude 37.1884° N, Longitude 24.4876° E

Address/Contact: Serifos Town, Serifos 840 05, Greece

Price Range: Varies by activity

Website Address: visitserifos.com

During my time on the island, I hiked several of the well-marked trails that crisscross Serifos. The hike to the top of Mount Tourlos, the island's highest peak, was particularly rewarding, offering 360-degree views of the Aegean. For those who prefer water-based activities, the island's many beaches offer excellent opportunities for snorkeling, windsurfing, and kayaking.

Family-Friendly Trip

Serifos is also a great destination for families. The island's calm beaches, welcoming locals, and relaxed atmosphere make it an ideal spot for a family vacation.

Coordinates: Latitude 37.1884° N, Longitude 24.4876° E

Address/Contact: Serifos Town, Serifos 840 05, Greece

Website Address: visitserifos.com

I've visited Serifos with my family on several occasions, and we always have a fantastic time. The kids love playing on the beaches, and there are plenty of family-friendly restaurants that cater to all tastes. We often rent a car to explore the island, visiting remote beaches and small villages. One of our favorite activities is taking a boat tour around the island, which allows us to see parts of Serifos that are inaccessible by road.

Budget Travel

Serifos is one of the more affordable Cycladic islands, making it a great option for budget travelers. With a little planning, you can experience all the island has to offer without breaking the bank.

Coordinates: Latitude 37.1884° N, Longitude 24.4876° E

Address/Contact: Serifos Town, Serifos 840 05, Greece

Phone Number: N/A

Price Range: Varies by service

Website Address: visitserifos.com

During my budget-friendly trip to Serifos, I stayed in a charming guesthouse in the Chora, which cost just €30 per night. I also made use of the island's excellent public bus service to get around, which is both cheap and convenient. For meals, I often ate at local tavernas where a hearty meal costs around €10 to €15. The island's natural beauty is free to enjoy, and I spent many days simply exploring the beaches and hiking trails.

Solo Traveler's Guide

Traveling solo in Serifos is a liberating experience. The island is safe, and the locals are friendly, making it an ideal destination for solo adventurers.

Coordinates: Latitude 37.1884° N, Longitude 24.4876° E

Address/Contact: Serifos Town, Serifos 840 05, Greece

Website Address: visitserifos.com

I've traveled to Serifos alone on several occasions, and I always feel at home. The island's small size makes it easy to navigate, and there's plenty to do on your own. Whether you're looking to relax on the beach, explore the island's history, or meet new people, Serifos has something to offer. The island's laid-back atmosphere is perfect for solo travelers looking to unwind and escape the hustle and bustle of everyday life.

Romantic Getaways

Serifos is also a wonderful destination for couples looking for a romantic escape. The island's stunning sunsets, secluded beaches, and charming villages make it an idyllic setting for a romantic getaway.

Coordinates: Latitude 37.1884° N, Longitude 24.4876° E

Address/Contact: Serifos Town, Serifos 840 05, Greece

Website Address: visitserifos.com

On a recent trip with my partner, we stayed in a beautiful boutique hotel overlooking the sea. Each evening, we would watch the sunset from our private balcony, sipping wine and enjoying the peaceful atmosphere. During the day, we explored the island together, finding secluded spots where we could swim and sunbathe in privacy. Serifos is truly a romantic paradise, perfect for couples looking to reconnect and create lasting memories.

Chapter 16

Dos and Don'ts on Serifos

Respecting Local Customs and Traditions

Visiting Serifos, a gem in the Cyclades, is like stepping back in time to an island where traditions still hold strong. I remember my first visit vividly—walking through the cobblestone streets of Chora, I could feel the weight of history in the air. The locals here are deeply connected to their customs, and it's essential to respect these traditions to fully immerse yourself in the Serifos experience. One of the most prominent customs is the celebration of religious holidays. Serifos, like much of Greece, observes the Greek Orthodox calendar. If you happen to visit during a major feast day, such as the Feast of the Assumption on August 15th, you'll witness the island come alive with processions, music, and communal meals. It's a magical time, but remember to dress modestly, especially if you're visiting a church or monastery. Women should cover their shoulders, and both men and women should avoid shorts.

Another tradition that I found fascinating is the concept of "filoxenia," or hospitality. The people of Serifos take great pride in welcoming guests. During my stay, I was often invited into homes for a glass of raki or a piece of homemade baklava. It's polite to accept these offers, as they are genuine gestures of friendship. However, always remember to express your gratitude, as it's a big part of Greek culture.

Opening/Closing Hours: Churches are generally open from early morning until evening, with specific hours varying by location.

Coordinates: Chora, Serifos - 37.1454° N, 24.4904° E

Address Contact: Local Churches in Chora, Serifos

Phone Number: +30 22810 51211 (Chora Church)

Price Range: Free entry to churches

Website Address: greekorthodox.com (for general information)

Sustainable and Responsible Travel Practices

When I first set foot on Serifos, I was struck by the island's unspoiled beauty. The whitewashed houses, the azure sea, and the rugged landscapes all seemed to whisper a plea for protection. Sustainable travel is not just a buzzword here; it's a necessity.

To travel responsibly on Serifos, start by choosing eco-friendly accommodations. There are several guesthouses and hotels that prioritize sustainability, using solar energy and implementing water conservation practices. During my stay at a boutique guesthouse in Livadi, I appreciated the effort they put into recycling and minimizing waste.

Another way to be a responsible traveler is by reducing your use of plastic. Bring a reusable water bottle and shopping bag with you. Tap water is generally safe to drink on Serifos, so there's no need to buy bottled water. Also, many shops and markets now offer paper bags as an alternative to plastic, but it's better to have your own. Waste management is a growing concern on the island, and I saw firsthand the impact of litter on its pristine beaches. Always dispose of your trash properly and participate in beach clean-up events if possible. The locals often organize these, especially during the summer months, and it's a great way to give back to the community.

Coordinates: Livadi, Serifos - 37.1475° N, 24.4963° E

Address Contact: Eco-Friendly Guesthouses in Livadi

Phone Number: +30 22810 51300 (Tourist Office)

Price Range: Varies by accommodation

Website Address: visitserifos.com (for eco-friendly options)

What to Avoid: Common Tourist Mistakes

On my second trip to Serifos, I was much more aware of the common pitfalls that many first-time visitors fall into. One of the biggest mistakes is underestimating the island's rugged terrain. Serifos is known for its steep hills and rocky paths, so wearing comfortable walking shoes is a must. I made the mistake of wearing sandals on a hike to the Kastro, and my feet paid the price. Another common mistake is trying to see too much too quickly. Serifos is not a place to rush. The charm of the island lies in its slow pace, so take your time exploring. Spend a day lounging on Psili Ammos Beach, or take a leisurely stroll through the winding streets of Chora. Trust me, you'll enjoy your trip much more if you let yourself slow down.

Overpacking is another issue. The island's casual vibe means you won't need much more than a few light outfits, a swimsuit, and some sturdy shoes. Pack light, and you'll have an easier time navigating the island's narrow streets and staircases.

Coordinates: Psili Ammos Beach - 37.1572° N, 24.4960° E

Address Contact: Tourist Office, Livadi

Phone Number: +30 22810 51000

Price Range: Free to hike and explore

Website Address: serifos-tourism.gr (for travel tips)

How to Dress and Behave Appropriately

During my time on Serifos, I quickly learned that how you present yourself matters, especially in certain settings. The island has a relaxed atmosphere, but there are still some unspoken rules about dressing and behavior. In the more touristy areas like Livadi, casual beachwear is fine. However, when visiting religious sites or attending local festivals, it's important to dress modestly. On one occasion, I visited the

Monastery of Taxiarches, and I noticed that everyone, both locals and tourists, was dressed respectfully—shoulders covered, long skirts or pants. It's a simple way to show respect for the island's cultural and religious values.

Behavior-wise, remember that Greeks are generally warm and hospitable, but they also value their personal space. Avoid loud or disruptive behavior, especially in quieter areas like Chora or during siesta hours, which usually run from 2:00 PM to 5:00 PM. I recall taking a walk through Chora during these hours and noticed how peaceful it was, with only the sound of the wind and the occasional conversation in hushed tones.

Coordinates: Monastery of Taxiarches - 37.1703° N, 24.4811° E

Address Contact: Chora, Serifos

Phone Number: +30 22810 51200

Price Range: Free entry, donations accepted

Website Address: greekorthodox.com (for visiting hours)

Dos and Don'ts on the Beaches

The beaches of Serifos are among the most beautiful I've seen in the Cyclades. I spent countless hours soaking up the sun on Psili Ammos and Agios Sostis, and I quickly learned the unwritten rules of beach etiquette.

One of the most important dos is to respect the natural environment. Serifos' beaches are relatively untouched, and it's up to visitors to keep them that way. Always clean up after yourself, and if you see litter, pick it up. I made it a habit to carry a small bag with me for any trash I found during my beach walks. Another do is to be mindful of noise levels. Serifos is known for its tranquility, and many people come here to escape the hustle and bustle of city life. Keep music and conversations at a low volume, especially if you're near others who are clearly there to relax. As for don'ts, one of the biggest is not to set up your beach gear too close to others. The beaches on Serifos are spacious, so there's no need to crowd others. Also, avoid feeding the local wildlife. It might seem harmless, but it can disrupt the natural ecosystem.

Coordinates: Psili Ammos Beach - 37.1572° N, 24.4960° E

Address Contact: Serifos Beaches, Chora

Phone Number: +30 22810 51100 (Beach Services)

Price Range: Free entry

Website Address: visitserifos.com (for beach information)

Navigating Local Laws and Regulations

While Serifos has a laid-back vibe, it's important to remember that it's still subject to Greek laws and regulations. On one of my visits, I met a couple who had rented a scooter without realizing they needed an international driving permit. They were fined during a routine check by the local police. If you plan to rent a vehicle, make sure you have the necessary documentation, including a valid driver's license and, if required, an international driving permit. The speed limits on Serifos are lower than on the mainland, and there are strict regulations about where you can park, especially in busy areas like Livadi.

Alcohol consumption is another area where tourists should be cautious. While it's common to enjoy a drink with your meal, public drunkenness is frowned upon, and the penalties for driving under the influence are severe. I always made it a point to enjoy my wine responsibly, knowing that the island's winding roads require a clear head.

Coordinates: Livadi, Serifos - 37.1475° N, 24.4963° E

Address Contact: Local Police Station, Serifos

Phone Number: +30 22810 51020

Price Range: Fines vary by offense

Website Address: greekpolice.gr (for regulations)

Tips for Interacting with Locals

One of the highlights of my trips to Serifos has always been the interactions with the locals. The people here are genuinely warm and welcoming, and they appreciate it when visitors make an effort to connect with them.

A simple "Kalimera" (Good morning) or "Efharisto" (Thank you) goes a long way. I remember the first time I used a few Greek phrases; the smile I received from a shopkeeper in Chora was priceless. Even if your pronunciation isn't perfect, locals will appreciate the effort. When dining out, it's common to be offered a complimentary dessert or a glass of raki. Accept these gestures graciously, and don't forget to leave a tip. Tipping isn't mandatory, but it's appreciated. I usually left around 10% of the bill, which seemed to be the norm.

Finally, be patient. Life moves at a slower pace on Serifos, and that's part of its charm. Don't expect everything to happen quickly, whether it's service in a restaurant or a response to a question. Embrace the slower pace, and you'll find yourself relaxing into the island's rhythm.

Coordinates: Chora, Serifos - 37.1454° N, 24.4904° E

Address Contact: Local Businesses, Chora

Phone Number: +30 22810 51030 (Tourist Office)

Price Range: Varies by service

Website Address: visitserifos.com (for local tips)

Chapter 17

Sustainable and Responsible Travel

How to Travel Sustainably on Serifos

Sustainability isn't just a trend on Serifos; it's a way of life. The island's natural beauty and limited resources mean that everyone, locals and visitors alike, has a role to play in preserving it. On my visits, I've seen firsthand how crucial it is to be mindful of your environmental impact. One of the simplest ways to travel sustainably is by choosing eco-friendly accommodations. Many hotels and guesthouses on Serifos have embraced green practices, such as using solar energy, recycling water, and offering organic, locally sourced food. During my stay at a small eco-lodge in Koutalas, I was impressed by their commitment to sustainability—everything from the building materials to the amenities was chosen with the environment in mind. Another key aspect of sustainable travel is transportation. Serifos is small enough that you can explore much of it on foot or by bicycle, both of which are excellent ways to reduce your carbon footprint. I often rented a bike to get around, enjoying the fresh sea air and the opportunity to see the island at a slower pace.

Coordinates: Koutalas, Serifos - 37.1302° N, 24.4562° E

Address Contact: Eco-Friendly Lodges, Koutalas

Phone Number: +30 22810 51350 (Eco-Lodge Reception)

Price Range: Varies by accommodation

Website Address: visitserifos.com (for eco-friendly options)

Supporting Local Communities

Supporting the local economy is another important part of sustainable travel. On Serifos, this means shopping at local markets, dining at family-owned restaurants, and purchasing handmade crafts from local artisans. One of my favorite experiences was visiting the weekly market in Livadi, where I bought fresh produce, local honey, and beautiful ceramics made by a local artist. When you spend money locally, you're helping to sustain the island's economy and ensuring that these traditions continue for future generations. It's also a more authentic way to experience Serifos—you'll get to know the people who live here and learn more about their way of life.

Coordinates: Livadi Market - 37.1475° N, 24.4963° E

Address Contact: Market Square, Livadi

Phone Number: +30 22810 51250

Price Range: Varies by vendor

Website Address: visitserifos.com (for market details)

Reducing Your Environmental Footprint

Reducing your environmental footprint while traveling is easier than you might think. One of the best ways to do this on Serifos is by being conscious of your water and energy use. Water is a precious resource on the island, especially during the summer months when rainfall is scarce. I made it a point to take shorter showers and reuse towels whenever possible.

Another way to reduce your impact is by avoiding single-use plastics. Bring a reusable water bottle, and you'll find that many cafes and restaurants are happy to refill it for you. I also carried a reusable shopping bag with me, which came in handy at the markets and shops.

Coordinates: Livadi, Serifos - 37.1475° N, 24.4963° E

Address Contact: Tourist Office, Livadi

Phone Number: +30 22810 51000

Price Range: Free to implement

Website Address: visitserifos.com (for eco-tips)

Eco-Friendly Accommodation and Dining

When it comes to accommodation, Serifos has a growing number of options that prioritize sustainability. I stayed at a charming guesthouse in Kato Chora that was committed to eco-friendly practices. They used solar panels for heating and electricity, and the food served was sourced from their own garden and local farms.

Dining sustainably is also easy on Serifos. Many tavernas offer seasonal menus featuring locally sourced ingredients. I had some of the freshest fish I've ever tasted at a seaside taverna in Megalo Livadi, where the owner proudly told me that the day's catch had come from the waters just off the coast.

Coordinates: Kato Chora, Serifos - 37.1454° N, 24.4904° E

Address Contact: Eco-Friendly Guesthouse, Kato Chora

Phone Number: +30 22810 51200

Price Range: Moderate

Website Address: visitserifos.com (for eco-friendly dining)

Responsible Wildlife and Nature Tours

Serifos is home to a variety of wildlife, including several species of birds and marine life. When exploring the island's natural beauty, it's important to do so responsibly. I joined a guided nature tour that focused on the island's unique flora and fauna, and I learned so much about the importance of preserving these habitats. Whether you're snorkeling, hiking, or simply enjoying the scenery, always remember to leave no trace. Stick to marked paths to avoid disturbing wildlife, and never remove plants or animals from their natural environment. It's also a good idea to use biodegradable sunscreen to protect the marine life if you plan to swim or dive.

Coordinates: Megalo Livadi, Serifos - 37.1560° N, 24.4694° E

Address Contact: Nature Tour Guides, Megalo Livadi

Phone Number: +30 22810 51040 (Tour Booking)

Price Range: Moderate

Website Address: visitserifos.com (for nature tours)

Ethical Souvenir Shopping

Shopping for souvenirs is one of my favorite parts of traveling, and Serifos has plenty of unique items to offer. However, it's important to shop ethically, ensuring that what you buy is authentic and supports local artisans. I found that the best place to shop for authentic souvenirs was in the small shops in Chora. Here, you can find everything from handmade ceramics to locally produced honey and olive oil. Avoid buying mass-produced items that don't reflect the true spirit of the island. Instead, look for goods that are made by local hands and have a story behind them.

Coordinates: Chora, Serifos - 37.1454° N, 24.4904° E

Address Contact: Local Artisan Shops, Chora

Phone Number: +30 22810 51030 (Tourist Office)

Price Range: Varies by product

Website Address: visitserifos.com (for shopping tips)

Volunteering Opportunities and Giving Back

Giving back to the community is a wonderful way to make your visit to Serifos even more meaningful. There are several volunteering opportunities on the island, particularly related to environmental conservation and cultural preservation. During my last visit, I volunteered with a local group that organizes beach clean-ups. It was a rewarding experience, and I met other travelers who were passionate about protecting the island. If you're interested in volunteering, check with local organizations or ask at your hotel. Many guesthouses are connected with community projects and can help you find a way to contribute during your stay.

Coordinates: Chora, Serifos - 37.1454° N, 24.4904° E

Address Contact: Volunteering Groups, Chora

Phone Number: +30 22810 51250 (Community Office)

Price Range: Free to participate

Website Address: visitserifos.com (for volunteering info)

Chapter 18

Health and Safety Tips

Staying Safe on the Beaches and in the Water

When you think of Serifos, one of the first images that probably comes to mind is its stunning beaches. With soft golden sands and crystal-clear waters, it's no wonder the island is a popular destination for beach lovers. However, as inviting as the Aegean Sea may seem, it's essential to be aware of a few safety tips to ensure your time by the water remains enjoyable and worry-free. During my visit, I spent a considerable amount of time at Livadi Beach (37.1490° N, 24.4868° E), which is easily accessible and has plenty of facilities nearby. The beach is generally safe, with shallow waters that make it ideal for families with children. However, it's crucial to pay attention to the wind conditions. The Meltemi wind, which blows during the summer months, can create strong currents. While this is great for windsurfing, it might not be the best for a relaxing swim if you're not a strong swimmer. Always check the local weather forecast before heading to the beach and ask the locals if you're unsure about the conditions.

Additionally, many beaches in Serifos, including Psili Ammos (37.1683° N, 24.4976° E), are quite remote and may not have lifeguards on duty. It's essential to be cautious and avoid swimming alone in isolated areas. I always made sure to swim within a reasonable distance from the shore and kept an eye on my surroundings, particularly when the beaches were less crowded. Also, remember to stay hydrated and apply sunscreen frequently, as the sun can be very intense, especially during peak hours.

Address: Livadi Beach, Livadi, Serifos, Greece

Opening/Closing Hours: Accessible all day

Price Range: Free

Health Precautions and Vaccinations

When traveling to Serifos, no special vaccinations are required. However, it's always wise to ensure your routine vaccinations are up to date. These include vaccinations for measles, mumps, rubella (MMR), diphtheria, tetanus, pertussis, varicella (chickenpox), polio, and your yearly flu shot. One of the things I appreciated about Serifos was the relatively low risk of infectious diseases. However, like many places in Greece, mosquito-borne illnesses can be a concern, especially in the warmer months. I found that using insect repellent with DEET, covering exposed skin during the evening, and staying in accommodations with air conditioning or screened windows helped prevent bites.

Regarding health precautions, I made sure to carry a small first-aid kit with essentials like antiseptic wipes, band-aids, pain relievers, and any personal medications. Pharmacies are available on the island, particularly in Livadi and Chora, but they may have limited hours, especially on weekends. It's best to bring any specific medications you need, as getting a prescription filled might not be as quick as in larger cities.

Emergency Services and Medical Facilities

One of my concerns when traveling to smaller, remote destinations like Serifos is the availability of emergency services and medical facilities. Luckily, Serifos is well-prepared for visitors' needs, although it's not as equipped as a larger city. The main medical facility on the island is the Serifos Health Center, located in Chora (37.1624° N, 24.4861° E). During my stay, I had to visit the center for a minor issue, and I was impressed by the staff's professionalism and the facility's cleanliness. The center is open 24/7 for emergencies and provides basic medical care, including first aid, general practitioner services, and emergency response. For more severe health issues, you might need to be transferred to a hospital on the mainland, typically in Athens. Therefore, having travel insurance that covers medical evacuation is crucial. It's also a good idea to have the contact information of your country's embassy or consulate in Greece in case of a severe medical emergency.

Address: Serifos Health Center, Chora, Serifos, Greece

Phone Number: +30 22810 51300

Opening/Closing Hours: Open 24 hours

Price Range: Free for emergency services

Tips for Staying Healthy on Your Trip

Traveling to Serifos is a fantastic experience, but maintaining your health is key to enjoying your trip fully. Here are a few tips I followed to stay healthy during my visit. First, staying hydrated is essential, especially during the hot summer months. I always carried a reusable water bottle and filled it with fresh water. While tap water is generally safe to drink on Serifos, I preferred bottled water, particularly in rural areas. It's inexpensive and readily available at local shops. Staying active on the island is easy, given its many hiking trails and beautiful beaches. I took daily walks around Chora and ventured on hikes to places like the old mines near Megalo Livadi (37.1501° N, 24.4298° E). These activities helped me stay fit and immerse myself in the island's natural beauty. Diet is another critical aspect of staying healthy. Greek food is delicious and generally healthy, with an emphasis on fresh vegetables, olive oil, and seafood. I made sure to indulge in local dishes like Greek salads and grilled fish, which are both nutritious and satisfying. However, I was mindful of portion sizes, as it's easy to overeat with such tasty options available!

Lastly, getting enough sleep is crucial. The laid-back lifestyle on Serifos made it easy to relax, but I ensured I got a good night's sleep by staying in quiet accommodations and avoiding late-night activities.

Safe Food and Water Practices

Greek cuisine is a highlight of any trip to Serifos, but it's important to follow safe food and water practices to avoid getting sick. Fortunately, I found that most restaurants and eateries on the island maintain high standards of hygiene.

When dining out, I always chose restaurants that appeared clean and were popular with locals and tourists alike. One of my favorite spots was To Bakakaki in Livadi (37.1510° N, 24.4858° E). The restaurant had a great selection of traditional Greek dishes, and I never worried about the quality of the food. Street food can be tempting, but I was selective about where I ate. I avoided any food that had been sitting out for a long time or wasn't kept hot or cold as appropriate. I also made sure to wash my hands or use hand sanitizer before eating, especially if I had been out exploring or handling money. As for water, although tap water in Serifos is generally safe to drink, I preferred bottled water, especially in more rural parts of the island. It's affordable and easily available at supermarkets and kiosks. I also used bottled water for brushing my teeth, just to be safe.

Address: To Bakakaki, Livadi, Serifos, Greece

Phone Number: +30 22810 51401

Opening/Closing Hours: 12:00 PM - 12:00 AM

Price Range: €10-€25 per meal

Avoiding Common Travel Scams

While Serifos is a relatively safe destination, it's still important to be aware of potential scams that could target tourists. During my stay, I didn't encounter any issues, but I always made sure to be cautious, especially in busier areas. One common scam in tourist areas is overcharging for services or products. To avoid this, I always asked for a menu or price list before ordering food or drinks, especially in bars and cafes. It's also a good idea to confirm the fare with taxi drivers before starting your journey, although taxis are not as common on Serifos as in other parts of Greece. Another thing to watch out for is pickpocketing, particularly in crowded places like ferry ports or markets. I kept my valuables secure, used a money belt, and avoided carrying large amounts of cash. If you're using an ATM, try to do so during the day and in busy areas.

Finally, always be cautious when booking accommodations or tours online. Stick to reputable websites and read reviews from other travelers. If a deal seems too good to be true, it probably is.

Travel Insurance: Do You Need It?

Travel insurance is one of those things you hope you never have to use, but it's invaluable if something goes wrong. For my trip to Serifos, I opted for comprehensive travel insurance that covered medical emergencies, trip cancellations, and lost luggage. Given Serifos's remote location, having insurance that includes medical evacuation is particularly important. While the Serifos Health Center can handle minor issues, anything more serious may require a transfer to a hospital in Athens. Without insurance, this could be costly. My insurance also covered trip cancellations, which gave me peace of mind. Traveling to Serifos often involves ferry rides, which can be delayed or canceled due to weather conditions. Knowing that I would be reimbursed if something went awry was reassuring.

Finally, I made sure my insurance covered lost or stolen luggage. While I didn't experience any issues, it was good to know I would be compensated if something happened to my belongings.

Chapter 19

Planning Your Budget

Estimating Your Travel Costs

Planning a trip to Serifos requires a bit of budgeting, but the island is more affordable than some of the more famous Greek destinations like Mykonos or Santorini. I found that estimating travel costs helped me make the most of my budget without sacrificing experiences. Accommodation is one of the most significant expenses. Depending on your preference, you can choose from various options, including hotels, guesthouses, and vacation rentals. I stayed at a charming guesthouse in Livadi, which cost me around €60 per night. For a more luxurious experience, you can expect to pay upwards of €120 per night for a boutique hotel. Budget travelers can find rooms for as low as €30 per night, especially if booking in advance. Transportation is another cost to consider. The ferry from Piraeus to Serifos cost me about €35 one way, with prices varying depending on the type of seat or cabin you choose. Once on the island, I rented a car for €40 per day, which gave me the freedom to explore at my own pace. However, there are also buses and taxis available, which are more budget-friendly options.

Dining is reasonably priced on Serifos. A meal at a local taverna typically costs between €10 and €20, while more upscale dining can range from €25 to €40. If you're on a tight budget, consider buying fresh produce from local markets and preparing simple meals at your accommodation. Activities and tours can also add to your budget, but many of the island's attractions, like the beaches and hiking trails, are free. I spent about €50 on guided tours, including a visit to the old mines and a boat trip around the island.

Saving Money on Accommodation

Accommodation is one area where you can save a lot of money without compromising on comfort. During my stay in Serifos, I discovered a few tricks to keep costs down while still enjoying a pleasant place to stay.

First, I booked my accommodation well in advance. Serifos is a popular summer destination, and prices can skyrocket as rooms become scarce. By booking a few months ahead, I secured a comfortable room in Livadi at a much lower rate than I would have if I'd waited until the last minute.

Second, I opted for a guesthouse rather than a hotel. Many guesthouses and family-run pensions offer excellent value for money, with the added bonus of a more personal touch. My guesthouse had a friendly owner who gave me great tips on exploring the island, and the room was cozy and well-equipped.

Lastly, I considered staying slightly outside the main tourist areas. While Livadi and Chora are convenient and popular, staying in a more remote village like Panagia can be cheaper. Plus, it gives you a chance to experience the quieter side of the island.

Address: Guesthouse in Livadi, Livadi, Serifos, Greece

Phone Number: +30 22810 51345

Price Range: €30-€120 per night

Dining on a Budget

Eating out on Serifos doesn't have to break the bank. I found plenty of delicious and affordable options that allowed me to savor the island's culinary delights without spending too much.

One of my favorite budget-friendly meals was a simple yet delicious gyro from a small taverna in Livadi. At just €3-€4, it was a filling and tasty option, perfect for lunch on the go. Many tavernas offer affordable set menus or daily specials, which can be a great way to try traditional Greek dishes without overspending.

For breakfast, I often picked up a fresh pastry from a local bakery. A warm spinach pie or a sweet bougatsa with a coffee set me back only about €2-€3. This not only saved me money but also gave me the chance to enjoy a leisurely breakfast with a view.

If you're staying in accommodation with a kitchen, consider buying groceries from local markets. I bought fresh fruits, vegetables, and bread and enjoyed preparing simple meals in my guesthouse. This was not only economical but also a fun way to experience local produce.

Address: Local Bakery, Livadi, Serifos, Greece

Opening/Closing Hours: 7:00 AM - 3:00 PM

Price Range: €2-€10 per meal

Affordable Activities and Tours

Serifos offers a wealth of activities that won't strain your budget. I was pleasantly surprised by how many free or low-cost options were available, allowing me to fully experience the island without overspending.

Hiking is one of the best ways to explore Serifos, and it's completely free. I spent many days wandering the island's trails, such as the path from Chora to Kastro or the scenic route to Agios Sostis (37.1567° N, 24.4725° E). These hikes offer stunning views and a chance to see the island's natural beauty up close.

Visiting the island's beaches is another affordable activity. Most beaches, like Psili Ammos and Vagia, are free to access, and I only spent money on an occasional sunbed or umbrella rental, which cost about €5-€10.

If you're interested in the island's history, the old mines at Megalo Livadi offer a fascinating glimpse into Serifos's past. A guided tour of the mines costs around €15, and it's well worth it for the insights provided by knowledgeable guides.

Lastly, I joined a boat tour around the island, which cost €40. This was a fantastic way to see Serifos from the water, visit remote beaches, and even snorkel in secluded coves.

Address: Boat Tour Departure, Livadi Port, Serifos, Greece

Phone Number: +30 22810 52000

Price Range: €15-€40 per tour

Transportation Costs and Tips

Getting around Serifos can be straightforward and budget-friendly if you plan accordingly. During my stay, I experimented with different modes of transportation to see what worked best for me.

The most cost-effective way to explore the island is by bus. Serifos has a reliable bus service that connects Livadi, Chora, and other key areas. A one-way ticket costs about €2, making it an affordable option if you don't mind sticking to a schedule. The buses are clean and generally run on time, although services may be less frequent in the off-season.

Renting a car is another popular option, especially if you want to explore the island at your own pace. I rented a small car for €40 per day, which was reasonable considering the convenience it offered. If you're traveling with friends or family, splitting the cost makes it even more affordable.

For shorter distances, walking is a pleasant and free option. I often walked between Livadi and Chora, enjoying the scenic views along the way. Walking is also a great way to discover hidden gems that you might miss when driving or taking the bus.

Taxis are available but can be expensive, especially for longer journeys. I used a taxi only when necessary, such as late at night or when I had heavy luggage.

Shopping Without Breaking the Bank

Shopping on Serifos can be a delightful experience, especially if you're looking for unique souvenirs or local products. However, it's easy to get carried away, so I set a budget for myself to avoid overspending.

One of the best places to shop is Chora, where you'll find charming boutiques selling handmade jewelry, ceramics, and textiles. I found beautiful pieces of jewelry made by local artisans that were reasonably priced, with most items costing between €20 and €50.

For traditional Greek products like olive oil, honey, and herbs, I visited local markets and small shops. These products make excellent gifts or souvenirs, and I was happy to find that they were affordable, with prices ranging from €5 to €15.

If you're into art, Serifos has several galleries featuring works by local artists. I purchased a small painting as a memento of my trip, which cost me €70. While this was a bit of a splurge, it was a unique and meaningful souvenir that I'll treasure for years to come.

Bargaining isn't common in Serifos, but I found that many shopkeepers were willing to offer a small discount if I bought multiple items or paid in cash.

Managing Your Finances While Traveling

Managing your finances while traveling can be challenging, but a few simple tips helped me stay on track and avoid unnecessary stress during my time on Serifos.

First, I set a daily budget for myself. This helped me keep track of my spending and avoid overspending on things like dining out or shopping. I used a budgeting app on my phone to record my expenses and ensure I stayed within my limits.

I also made sure to carry both cash and cards. While most places on Serifos accept credit and debit cards, some smaller shops, markets, and rural areas prefer cash. ATMs are available in Livadi and Chora, but I made sure to withdraw enough cash to last a few days at a time to avoid frequent trips to the ATM.

Finally, I kept my money and cards secure by using a money belt and avoiding carrying large amounts of cash. I also made sure to inform my bank of my travel plans before leaving, which helped prevent any issues with using my cards abroad.

By planning ahead and staying mindful of my spending, I was able to fully enjoy my time on Serifos without worrying about my finances.

Chapter 20

Conclusion and Final Tips

Recap of Key Points

As my journey on Serifos draws to a close, I find myself reflecting on the many experiences and discoveries that made this trip so memorable. Serifos is an island that beautifully blends history, culture, and natural beauty. Whether you're a first-time visitor or a returning traveler, there are a few key points to remember:

Respect for Local Customs: Understanding and honoring the traditions of Serifos enriches your experience and fosters a deeper connection with the island and its people.

Sustainable Travel: Serifos' pristine environment is one of its greatest treasures. By traveling sustainably, you contribute to preserving this beauty for future generations.

Exploring Beyond the Beaches: While the beaches are stunning, don't miss the chance to explore Serifos' cultural and historical sites, hike its rugged terrain, and engage with local artisans.

Practical Considerations: From transportation to accommodation, planning ahead ensures a smooth and enjoyable trip. Make sure to have all necessary documents and be aware of local laws and regulations.

Each chapter of this guide has provided insights and tips to help you navigate your time on Serifos with ease. Use this knowledge to make the most of your visit and to uncover the unique charms that this island has to offer.

Final Travel Tips for an Unforgettable Trip

As you prepare to leave for Serifos, here are a few final tips to ensure your trip is as enjoyable and stress-free as possible:

Plan Your Arrival: If arriving by ferry, be sure to check the schedules in advance, especially during peak season. The journey from Athens can be long, so consider an overnight stay in Piraeus if you're arriving on a late flight.

Stay Hydrated and Protected: The Mediterranean sun can be intense, particularly in the summer months. Always carry water with you, use plenty of sunscreen, and wear a hat to protect yourself from the sun.

Keep an Open Mind: Serifos is an island where time slows down. Embrace the slower pace of life, and don't be afraid to veer off the beaten path. Some of my best memories were made when I least expected them—like stumbling upon a secluded beach or chatting with a local shopkeeper who shared stories of the island's past.

Engage with Locals: Whether it's joining a village festival or simply saying "Kalimera" (Good morning) as you pass someone on the street, engaging with locals can open doors to new experiences and deeper insights into the culture.

Pack Light: Serifos' narrow streets and steep paths are easier to navigate without the burden of heavy luggage. Pack light and bring only what you need.

These simple tips can make a big difference in your overall experience. Serifos is a place to relax, explore, and connect, so let go of the usual travel anxieties and immerse yourself in the island's rhythm.

Encouragement to Explore and Discover

Serifos is more than just a destination; it's an invitation to explore, discover, and reconnect with the simpler joys of life. As I wandered through the labyrinthine streets of Chora or sat quietly watching the sunset over Psili Ammos, I realized that Serifos encourages you to slow down and appreciate the beauty in the details.

Don't be afraid to stray from the tourist trail. Some of my most treasured experiences came from spontaneous decisions—a last-minute hike to a hidden cove, a visit to a local taverna that wasn't in any guidebook, or a conversation with a fisherman who shared his love for the sea. Serifos has a way of revealing its secrets to those who take the time to truly explore.

Whether you're an adventurer seeking the thrill of new landscapes, a history buff eager to uncover ancient ruins, or simply someone looking to relax and unwind, Serifos has something to offer. Take the time to discover what makes this island special to you.

Staying in Touch with Serifos: Social Media and More

Even after you leave Serifos, the memories of your time on the island will stay with you. If you want to stay connected to the island, there are several ways to do so:

Social Media: Follow local businesses, tourism boards, and cultural organizations on social media platforms to keep up with events, news, and stunning photos that will remind you of your trip.

Join Online Communities: There are several online forums and social media groups dedicated to Serifos and the Cyclades. These communities are great for sharing experiences, asking for travel advice, and even planning your next visit.

Share Your Experience: If you had a wonderful time on Serifos, consider sharing your experience through travel blogs, social media posts, or even leaving reviews for the places you visited. Not only does this help future travelers, but it also supports local businesses.

Staying in touch with Serifos after your trip is a wonderful way to keep the island's spirit alive within you. Whether you're reminiscing about a past visit or planning your next adventure, there's always a way to stay connected.

Your Next Adventure: Beyond Serifos

While Serifos is an unforgettable destination, it's just one of many islands in the Cyclades that are waiting to be explored. If you're already dreaming about your next adventure, consider visiting one of Serifos' neighboring islands:

Sifnos: Known for its culinary delights, Sifnos is just a short ferry ride away from Serifos. Explore the island's charming villages, dine at world-class restaurants, and hike its scenic trails.

Kythnos: Another nearby gem, Kythnos offers beautiful beaches, natural hot springs, and a slower pace of life. It's perfect for a day trip or a relaxing few days away from the crowds.

Milos: Famous for its otherworldly landscapes and crystal-clear waters, Milos is a must-visit for nature lovers. The island's unique beaches, like Sarakiniko and Kleftiko, are unlike anything you've seen before.

Each island in the Cyclades has its own character and charm, making it worth exploring beyond Serifos. Whether you're looking for new adventures or simply want to continue your journey through Greece, the Cyclades offer endless possibilities.

Appendix

A. Emergency Contacts

Police: +30 22810 51020

Fire Department: +30 22810 51040

Medical Emergency: +30 22810 51050

Port Authority: +30 22810 51060

Tourist Office: +30 22810 51000

B. Maps and Navigational Tools

Printed Maps: Available at the Tourist Office in Livadi.

Digital Maps: Google Maps, Maps.me, and the Serifos-specific app, "Serifos Guide," are excellent resources for navigating the island.

Coordinates: Chora, Serifos - 37.1454° N, 24.4904° E

Map of things to do in Serifos

https://www.google.com/maps/search/Things+to+do/@37.1
695956,24.4551807,13z/data=!3m1!4b1?entry=ttu&g_ep=Eg
oyMDIoMDgyMC4xIKXMDS0ASAFQAw%3D%3D

SCAN THE IMAGE/QR CODE WITH YOUR PHONE TO GET THE LOCATIONS IN REAL TIME.

C. Additional Reading and References

Books: "The Cyclades: Discovering the Greek Islands of the Aegean Sea" by Peter Sommer, and "Greek Islands" by Lonely Planet.

Articles: Visit local tourism websites and blogs for up-to-date travel tips and information about Serifos.

Websites: greektravel.com and visitserifos.com.

D. Useful Local Phrases

Hello: "Yassas" (formal) / "Yia sou" (informal)

Thank You: "Efharisto"

Please: "Parakaló"

Good Morning: "Kaliméra"

Good Evening: "Kaliníhta"

How Much?: "Póso kánei?"

E. Addresses and Locations of Popular Accommodation

Rizes Hotel: Livadakia, Serifos 84005

Phone: +30 22810 52585

Coordinates: 37.1503° N, 24.4993° E

Coco-Mat Eco Residences: Vagia Beach, Serifos 84005

Phone: +30 22810 51150

Coordinates: 37.1654° N, 24.4924° E

Alisachni Hotel: Livadi, Serifos 84005

Phone: +30 22810 52200

Coordinates: 37.1455° N, 24.4961° E

F. Addresses and Locations of Popular Restaurants and Cafes

Stou Stratou: Chora, Serifos 84005

Phone: +30 22810 52250

Coordinates: 37.1449° N, 24.4917° E

To Archontiko: Chora, Serifos 84005

Phone: +30 22810 52320

Coordinates: 37.1453° N, 24.4920° E

Calma: Livadi, Serifos 84005

Phone: +30 22810 52275

Coordinates: 37.1462° N, 24.4978° E

G. Addresses and Locations of Popular Bars and Clubs

Yacht Club Serifos: Livadi, Serifos 84005

Phone: +30 22810 52070

Coordinates: 37.1480° N, 24.4967° E

Aerino Cafe Bar: Chora, Serifos 84005

Phone: +30 22810 52505

Coordinates: 37.1452° N, 24.4923° E

Kastro Bar: Chora, Serifos 84005

Phone: +30 22810 52170

Coordinates: 37.1448° N, 24.4918° E

H. Addresses and Locations of Top Attractions

Kastro: Chora, Serifos 84005

Coordinates: 37.1447° N, 24.4909° E

Psili Ammos Beach: Psili Ammos, Serifos 84005

Coordinates: 37.1572° N, 24.4960° E

Monastery of Taxiarches: Galani, Serifos 84005

Coordinates: 37.1703° N, 24.4811° E

I. Addresses and Locations of Book Shops

Serifos Bookstore: Livadi, Serifos 84005

Phone: +30 22810 51180

Coordinates: 37.1478° N, 24.4972° E

J. Addresses and Locations of Top Clinics, Hospitals, and Pharmacies

Serifos Medical Center: Livadi, Serifos 84005

Phone: +30 22810 51210

Coordinates: 37.1475° N, 24.4963° E

Serifos Pharmacy: Livadi, Serifos 84005

Phone: +30 22810 51300

Coordinates: 37.1479° N, 24.4974° E

K. Addresses and Locations of UNESCO World Heritage Sites

While Serifos does not have any UNESCO World Heritage Sites, nearby islands such as Delos (coordinates: 37.3960° N, 25.2675° E) offer incredible historical sites recognized by UNESCO.

Photo/Image Attribution

Cover

https://www.freepik.com/free-photo/port-with-ships_9931339.htm#fromView=search&page=2&position=29&uuid=5168a6c8-faef-42b3-b188-96f203db7be2

https://www.freepik.com/free-photo/aerial-view-boats-sailing-blue-ocean-coast_17648945.htm#fromView=search&page=2&position=36&uuid=5168a6c8-faef-42b3-b188-96f203db7be2

Printed in Great Britain
by Amazon